FACE

FACE VALUE

God in the Place of Encounter

◆

VANESSA HERRICK
& IVAN MANN

DARTON·LONGMAN+TODD

First published in 2002 by
Darton, Longman and Todd Ltd
1 Spencer Court
140–142 Wandsworth High Street
London SW18 4JJ

ISBN 0–232–52377–0

A catalogue record for this book is available from the British Library.

Designed by Sandie Boccacci
Set in 10.5/13.75pt Palatino
by Intype London Ltd
Printed and bound in Great Britain by
The Bath Press, Bath

♦

CONTENTS

♦

ACKNOWLEDGEMENTS

Books don't just happen – and those who have written them know the great debt that is often owed to the many people who, in diverse and sometimes unknowing ways, have contributed to them. So it is that we offer our thanks to all those with whom we have had conversations about transfiguration, from the book's genesis to its completion: to Kathy Dyke and Katie Worrall at DLT; to students and colleagues at Fitzwilliam College and Ridley Hall in Cambridge; and to the Great Yarmouth Team for their forbearance, humour and understanding. We are grateful too to those who have furnished us with stimulating material – often at just the right moment – and especially to Professor Colin Gunton of King's College, London; to Professor Graham Stanton, the Lady Margaret's Professor of Divinity at Cambridge; to Dr Rosemary Wright, Senior Lecturer in the School of Art at St Andrew's University; to the Revd Richard Ginn and to Iona Hine. Perhaps our greatest debt is to those close friends and family who have supported and encouraged us on the days when the task of writing alongside full-time responsibilities in college and parish has seemed impossible: to Jeremy Begbie, Graham Davies, Eilish Heath, Caroline Hallett, Jeffrey Carnell, David, Adam and Peter Herrick – thank you – for in your loving affirmation, we have glimpsed beyond 'face value', and seen the face of Christ.

May 2002

♦

FOREWORD

THERE CAN BE FEW things more vital to Christian understanding and living than simultaneously entering more
deeply into Scripture and into life today. There is in particular
a long tradition of entering into the 'mysteries' of Christian
faith from different angles and at different levels. In *Face
Value* Vanessa Herrick and Ivan Mann do this sensitively,
imaginatively and practically.

In choosing the Transfiguration they have identified a
pivotal moment in the Gospels of Matthew, Mark and Luke
that is largely neglected in Western Christianity. They explain
the neglect, and they also show in multiple ways how extraordinarily fruitful it is to meditate on this event. The themes
of knowing Christ, worship and fear, time and experience,
suffering, and obedience and discipleship are reflected upon
in ways that do justice to peak experiences, to ordinary life
and to the agonies, anguish, doubts, and ambiguities that
threaten to overwhelm us. There is a wide range of reference
and quotation woven into each chapter, distilling wisdom
from different traditions, periods and experiences.

There are many fine touches in this book. I especially
appreciated the way in which the theme of transfiguration
was deeply related both to the Old Testament and to the
Gospel of John, and also how the gentle shifts in focus convey

the truth that going deeper into the Bible is at the same time to go deeper simultaneously into God and into the world. The authors have done this sort of thing before in *Jesus Wept*; here they develop their striking talent for joint authorship in fresh ways.

By the end of this book one has been led through a thoughtful, well-crafted meditation on central matters of Christian faith and on their relevance to many areas of one's own life. Reading it in the week before 6 August I was left above all with two things: the biblical texts themselves, newly illuminated; and a sense that the mystery of the Transfiguration, already one of my favourite feasts, has the depth and breadth to come into its own in glorious ways in the twenty-first century.

DAVID F. FORD
31 July 2002

Chapter 1

♦

LOOKING BEYOND THE INTRODUCTION

W HEN WE BEGIN A BOOK we want to know what it is about. The title only helps us so far. We want to know more. In the same way, when we meet a person we want to get beyond the formal introduction and get to know something more about them. This book, focusing on the Transfiguration of Jesus, attempts to help us in the process of looking beyond the scriptural accounts of this event and so open ourselves to encountering God and ourselves afresh. As we do, we discover also that our encounters with other people and with situations may be encounters of deeper insight.

The Transfiguration is a defining moment in the life of Christ and in the lives of his disciples – not just for the three who were present but also for those other disciples who came to believe through their witness and through the witness of the Gospel. To approach Scripture as one of these disciples is to encounter God and to explore what it means to live in the light of that encounter. There can be no doubt that such an encounter may change our life and way of living far beyond the surface arrangement of our lives.

In this introductory chapter we look at what we mean by seeing beyond 'face value' and then reflect on defining moments in our lives and in the life of the world. We look at some such moments in the lives of individuals and then see what kind of impact they have and the response that they evoke. In following chapters we then begin to develop an understanding of the Transfiguration as a paradigm for encounters, and as a key to help us examine our response to such defining moments and how they determine our manner of living.

FACE VALUE

There are two ways of seeing life. We can look at the surface or we can look further. We can see the face value of a situation – what is presented to us – or we can give enough time and thought to see beyond what is apparent and discover more. Michel Quoist, for instance, looks at a banknote but sees more than money:

> Lord, you see this note, it frightens me.
> You know its secrets, you know its history.
> How heavy it is!
> It scares me for it cannot speak.
> It will never tell all it hides in its creases . . .

And then later in his prayer he lists some of its secrets:

> Through how many hands has it passed, Lord?
> And what has it done in the course of its long silent
> trips?
> It has offered white roses to the radiant fiancée.
> It has paid for the baptismal party and fed the growing
> baby.
> It has provided bread for the family table . . .
> But it has sent the letter breaking the engagement . . .
> It has brought the liquor that made the drunkard . . .
> It has produced the film unfit for children . . .
> It has bought for a few hours the body of a woman.

It has paid for the weapons of crime and the wood of the coffin . . .[1]

Quoist, writing in 1963, begins the process of seeing beyond the face value of the note to see its deeper meaning. In an age where image is sometimes emphasised above substance, to suggest that we look beyond face value is counter-cultural, and yet it is precisely what the Transfiguration account invites us to do. It invites us to look beyond the face of Jesus and see his deeper significance.

Inspiring as they are, it is all too easy to get carried away by high-flown phrases about Christ and about the Christian life. In a twelfth-century sermon Julian of Vezelay draws a beautiful image of Christ becoming man. He describes it as 'the moment when God's all-powerful Word would leave the tender embrace of the Father and come down into his mother's womb, bringing us the news of salvation.'[2]

What was heavenly became earthly and had to be worked out in the earthliness of the pregnancy of Mary and in the parental skills of both Mary and Joseph. The 'beautiful image' had to be lived out in Jesus' hidden ministry and then in his public ministry, his preaching and his passion, his living and dying and rising again. Here is both encounter with the mystery of God and the living out of the reality of that encounter.

DEFINING MOMENTS

A man was lying in a coma in an intensive care unit. Nothing would get through to him. After a month in the coma he suddenly and inexplicably took a turn for the worse. He was labelled as having no auditory response. It was at this stage that a music therapist was brought in to see him. She asked to be left alone with him and very gently began to sing with him, matching her singing to his breathing. As the sessions went on he began to respond, changing his breathing to see

3

whether the therapist would change her song. She did. There was communication: person was meeting person.

It is fascinating to read the patient's account of that time after his operation. He says it was like being on a battlefield in the Middle Ages, with death all around him and the only outcome for him. Then he writes:

> The point it all changed was when I first heard the music. The music was exquisite! The first time I didn't recognise it as a voice . . . but the second time I knew it was a voice, that there was a person there, there was someone who didn't want to kill me. I remember thinking, there is life, there is something else but this, there is someone who wants me to survive . . . and not only wants me, but is helping me to connect to life again.
>
> But every time people shouted at me I went back to the idea of dying. It was such a struggle to do anything, and when they shouted at me 'Open your eyes' ten times a day I thought 'I'm not in a circus!' I decided not to respond . . . The machines in the room I felt were bombs and weapons. But the music I felt was my music. I decided to live when I first heard the music . . .[3]

The music therapist had discovered that her task was to find a way of being alongside the patient, and so by making her song reflect his pulse and breathing, she made connections. She teaches us an important lesson – after all, she did not previously know the man, and yet she instinctively and directly approached him not as the victim of a cardiac arrest, nor as a husband or father or colleague, but simply as a person. She stroked his humanity by her song.

For the man her singing was a defining moment and his life was changed by it. For others defining moments may be less dramatic but none the less real. Monica Furlong, for instance, writes of an experience that we might all share – sitting at a bus stop:

During the two years just before and after I was twenty I had two experiences which led to religious conversion. The first occurred when I was waiting at a bus stop on a wet afternoon. It was opposite the Odeon cinema, outside a station, and I was surrounded by people, shops, cars. A friend was with me. All of a sudden, for no apparent reason, everything looked different. Everything I could see shone, vibrated, throbbed with joy and with meaning. I knew that it had done this all along, and would go on doing it, but that usually I couldn't see it. It was all over in a moment or two. I climbed on to the bus, saying nothing to my friend – it seemed impossible to explain – and sat stunned with astonishment and happiness ... The second experience occurred some months later ... I felt myself spoken to. I was aware of being regarded by love, of being wholly accepted, accused, forgiven, all at once. The joy of it was the greatest I had ever known in my life. I had been born for this moment and had marked time till it occurred.[4]

Such moments may be entirely related to our circumstances or may be clearly seen as having religious as well as spiritual significance.[5] It is said of St Benedict, for example, that

Through a balanced pattern of living and praying Benedict reached the point where he glimpsed the glory of God. Gregory recounts a vision that Benedict received towards the end of his life. In the dead of night he suddenly beheld a flood of light shining down from above more brilliant than the sun, and with it every trace of darkness cleared away. According to his own description, the whole world was gathered up before his eyes 'in what appeared to be a single ray of light'.[6]

Such defining moments have been experienced not only by the saints of old but also by modern-day Christians, as we have seen with Monica Furlong. They also happen to people who would not consider themselves as religious in the conventional sense. John McCarthy, for instance, writes of his time as a hostage in Lebanon:

> One morning these fears became unbearable. I stood in the cell sinking into despair. I felt that I was literally sinking, being sucked down into a whirlpool. I was on my knees, gasping for air, drowning in hopelessness and helplessness. I thought that I was passing out. I could only think of one thing to say – 'Help me please, oh God, help me.' The next instant I was standing up, surrounded by a warm bright light. I was dancing, full of joy. In the space of a minute, despair had vanished, replaced by boundless optimism.
>
> What had happened? I had never had any great faith, despite a Church of England upbringing. But I felt that I had to give thanks . . . It gave me great strength to carry on, and, more importantly, a huge renewal of hope – I was going to survive. Throughout my captivity I would take comfort from this experience . . .[7]

These moments in people's lives, which clearly have tremendous emotional and psychological significance for them, are experiences which they see as also having spiritual significance. But there are other moments when we become aware of being in the presence of wonder which need not be identified in the same way – moments of awe as we contemplate the natural world, or of terror as we watch events that both draw us by their power and yet repel us by their violence, brutality or naked evil. These are not so much about individuals but about events that touch whole communities, nations, or even the international community. Such moments in recent years may be recognised, for example, in the death of Diana, Princess of Wales, and in the destruction of the World Trade Centre in New York. Here are events of which it is too easily said that 'the world will never be the same again', and yet if the world is to be different, the impact of those events will need to shape personal attitudes, corporate resolve and the political will. The living out of such moments implies, then, a commitment both to the reality of the event and to its defining role. They are moments which may be signs of God's moment – times when God seeks to break in; but if so, they need to be recognised as such, an appropriate response must be made and a deep resolve for change needs to be nurtured.

Perhaps one example of how such resolve may effect change is to be found in South America, where

> In *We drink from our own wells*, for example, Gustavo Gutierrez chronicles the spiritual experience of those who, in South America, have heard and practised the good news of 'liberation'. For them, the death of exploitation and oppression has been transformed into the life of Christian fellowship and service. And this transformation is just as much a work of Christ as anything that he did during his ministry in Palestine. So far as they are concerned it provides striking evidence of who he was – and is.[8]

In these examples we see both the appropriation of a defining moment and the effectiveness of resolve. Such encounter with God and the reality of Christ is both a historical event and a present encounter, suggesting that the transfiguration experience can be both an instantaneous event and a process – something we explore further in Chapter 3.

GOD'S MOMENT

One way of distinguishing between 'defining moments' – encounters with trauma or joy which lift us beyond ourselves and give us fresh perspective – and these more overtly 'spiritual moments' would be to define the latter as 'God-moments'. Experience suggests that such moments are those when God breaks through the disjunctions of our existence.

It is as if God finds a 'chink' in our self-protective armour and gladly walks into our life in a new way. These 'chinks' are often our wounds[9] or peak experiences. In Jesus' life such moments were numerous – in particular we may suggest his Baptism, his Transfiguration, Gethsemane and his Passion, when Jesus placed himself into the hands of others or into the hand of the Father.

In our own prayer and life we too may experience such moments. We cannot make them happen. They happen to us. What we can do, in the light of the pattern in Jesus' life, is to be open to them, to become aware of them and recognise them. Then we can respond to the tragedies and triumphs of our lives – the agony and the ecstasy which come to us – in new ways, because we have our senses alive to the presence of God in them.

However, these moments when God chooses to make himself known may not be immediately revealed to us as 'God-moments'. It may be only with hindsight that we recognise them for what they are. Nor will they necessarily fill us with Monica Furlong's sense of 'being regarded by love, of being wholly accepted, accused, forgiven, all at once'. Instead they may fill us with apprehension and awe – even blind terror. There may be a sense of being completely out of control, and even a sense of 'breakdown' as our world-view collapses and another is reluctant to appear.

It is possible too that some defining moments may or may not become God-moments, depending on our response. In 1933, for instance, the young Hungarian physicist, Leo Szilard, was waiting for traffic lights near the British Museum to change. As the lights changed to green, 'Time cracked open before him and he saw a way into the future, death into the world and all our woe, the shape of things to come.'[10] It was then that he recognised the possibility of a self-sustaining chain reaction which would 'liberate energy on an industrial scale, and construct atomic bombs'.[11]

Moments of such revelation clearly need to be worked on and choices need to be made about how the knowledge and insight gained may be used for the good of humanity. Having our eyes opened so that sight gives way to insight is a gift, but beyond the gift is the use to which it is put and the higher ideal or power to which it is offered. So we are left with real questions about how any kind of spiritual experience is to be turned into the stuff of life. These are questions of allegiance and of our wider understanding and belief systems.

As we explore the Transfiguration we will see that these moments of revelation – which are, at times, glimpses into eternity – need to be contained within a framework of obedience and discipline. If our response to revelation is to be more than an emotional or spiritual one, it needs to be incarnational. That is, we need to have a means of holding what we have seen against our own belief system(s), the experience and knowledge of others (past and present), the needs and expectations of the wider community and our understanding of the God we serve.

This is the whole issue of 'discernment' where we both listen to the voices of our experience and also to other voices which will either confirm or challenge our understanding of what has happened until the meaning becomes clearer. This is a process of reflection and fact-gathering, of insight, intuition and study. It is a getting to grips with a double reality – the reality of revelation and the reality of life. Without it we can too easily become pious dreamers. With it we become saints – our feet firmly on earth and our eyes fixed on heaven. It is then that further transfiguring moments may happen. In Scripture, for example, such a double reality finds eloquent expression in the account of Stephen's martyrdom (Acts 7) where Stephen 'gazed into heaven and saw the glory of God' but was then stoned.

C. Day Lewis expresses a less dramatic but nonetheless powerful experience of this double reality in his poem 'A Privileged Moment':

Released from hospital, only half alive still,
Cautiously feeling the way back into himself,
Propped up in bed like a guy, he presently ventured
A glance at the ornaments on his mantelshelf.

White, Wedgwood blue, dark lilac coloured or ruby –
Things you could say, which had known their place and
    price,
Gleamed out at him with urgency of angels
Eager for him to see through their disguise.

Slowly he turned his head. By gust-flung snatches
A shower announced itself on the windowpane;
He saw unquestioning, not even astonished,
Handfuls of diamonds sprung from a dazzling chain.

Gently at last the angels settled back now
Into mere ornaments, the unearthly sheen
And spill of diamond into familiar raindrops.
It was enough. He'd seen what he had seen.[12]

Those last words, 'He'd seen what he had seen', could be the epitaph of many of the early disciples. They remind us of Mary's words, 'I have seen the Lord' (John 20:18); of Paul's vision on the Damascus Road (Acts 22:6); of Peter's statement, 'we had been eyewitnesses of his majesty' (2 Peter 1:16); and of John's proclamation of what he had seen and heard (1 John 1:1).

These are the transfiguring moments. They mark the beginning of a changed life. In the next two chapters we look at the history of the Transfiguration in the life of the Church and then at 'transfiguration moments' in Scripture.

Chapter 2

♦

A FORGOTTEN
FEAST

THE TRANSFIGURATION IS ONE OF the most extraordinary stories in the Gospels: mountain-top visions of Jesus, in robes which the soap-powder companies would pay millions for, standing chatting with the long-gone Moses and Elijah, mysterious clouds and a thundering voice. Small wonder that Peter, James and John fell to the ground and were overcome by fear. It's the stuff of Hitchcock and *Star Wars* and *Dr Who* all rolled into one.

Perhaps the most surprising thing is that this story made its way into the Gospels at all. After all, it was only attested by three disciples, and they could have been drunk or dreaming. Indeed, perhaps they imagined it all? Yet the early Church was so convinced of the importance of their experience, that for three of the four Gospel writers (and perhaps for Jesus himself), the Transfiguration was to become the turning point of the Gospel narrative and to take on meaning far beyond the description of the event itself.[1]

In this chapter, we shall ask why it is that over the centuries (in the Western Church at least), the Transfiguration has been a largely 'forgotten feast'. In the next, we shall go on to look at the Transfiguration *through the eyes of Peter*, allowing the Gospel narrative to illustrate his experience, and allowing us to begin to identify some of the key themes which emerge, and which demonstrate the Transfiguration to be a theological crossroads of enormous significance.

TRANSFIGURATION? WHAT'S THAT?

Since 1457, the Feast of the Transfiguration has been celebrated on 6 August – a date now 'marooned' in the middle of the long school holiday, when many churches are cruising gently through those 'quiet' summer weeks when nothing much is going on, and many regular members of the congregation are away. In the Church of England, the *ASB 1980* made provision for the Gospel account of the Transfiguration to be read on the fourth Sunday in Lent. Since, however, this particular Sunday is also 'Mothering Sunday', the set readings were often replaced with something more appropriate to the 'family' theme of the day's services. The result was that regular churchgoers often simply had very little idea of what the Transfiguration was about, and (like Trinity Sunday) many preachers looked for any excuse to avoid having to make sense of it! More recently, however, the *Common Worship Lectionary* has made provision for the reading of the Gospel of the Transfiguration on the Sunday next before Lent, (usually towards the end of February or the beginning of March), and congregations and preachers alike have had to begin to grapple with its place and significance in the Gospel narrative.

EAST AND WEST

It has not always been so – particularly in the Eastern tradition of the Christian Church. Only three of Jesus' disciples experienced the actual event. Yet it was clearly considered to be of great significance, not only for them personally, but for the life of the early Church as a whole – a significance demonstrated by its place at the heart of the Synoptic Gospels and by the reference in 2 Peter chapter 1.[2] Already in apostolic (and early post-apostolic) times, the Mount of Transfiguration had become known as the 'holy mount' (2 Peter 1:18). According to Origen, the mountain in question was Tabor,[3] a tradition also attested to by Cyril of Jerusalem[4] and Jerome[5] (although some scholars, including Michael Ramsey, have suggested that Mount Hermon was the likely locus of the event).

It is not known when the festival was first celebrated, but it was kept in Jerusalem as early as the seventh century, and in most parts of the Byzantine Empire by the ninth century. According to the Armenian bishop Gregory Arsharuni (c. 690), the origin of the feast lay with Gregory the Illuminator (d. 337), who substituted it for a pagan feast of Aphrodite.[6] Some scholars suggest, however, that it is more likely to have originated in the fourth[7] or fifth centuries, in place of a pagan nature-feast, somewhere in the highlands of Asia.[8] It was gradually introduced in the Western Church, and its observance was fixed on 6 August by Pope Callistus in 1457, as a thank-offering for a victory over the Turks at Belgrade on 6 August 1456.

Despite the slightly higher status given to the Transfiguration by the *Revised Common Lectionary*,[9] the Western Church still declines to attribute to it the prominence given to it in the Orthodox Churches, where it has always been one of the twelve major festivals.

The Syrians and Armenians (for whom the feast is preceded by a period of fasting) keep it on the seventh Sunday after Pentecost. In the Greek and Russian Churches it is accompanied by a vigil and an octave, and marked by a ceremony of blessing of fruits.

This difference of emphasis is also evident in the extent to which the Transfiguration has been depicted in Western art (especially painting and stained glass). Here, its appearance has become comparatively rare, especially since the sixteenth century and the Council of Trent. Important examples include that of Duccio de Buaninsegna and the illumination from John de Berry's *Petites Heures* – both from the fourteenth century;

and paintings by Fra Angelico, Bellini (two) and Perugino from the fifteenth century. In their structure these all depend heavily on Eastern iconography (see below), but each is presented in its contemporary 'flavour' of dress, architecture and environment. Perhaps the most famous (and the most interesting from our point of view) is the *Transfiguration* painted by Raphael in 1518–20, to which we shall refer in greater detail in the last chapter of this book.

By contrast, the Transfiguration has continued as a key focus for the depiction of events in the life of Christ in Eastern iconography, appearing as a 'standard' panel on the iconostasis of most Orthodox churches. Not only that, but because the whole task of painting icons is understood as 'painting with light', the Transfiguration is the very first subject that a new icon artist is required to paint.

In simple terms, the icon of the Transfiguration is depicted with three levels and operates with a double perspective. The levels are: at the top, representing the heavenly kingdom, Jesus standing on a mountain, with Moses and Elijah to right and left respectively, each sometimes standing on their 'own' mountains; in the middle, on either side, Jesus ascends and descends from the mountain, conversing with his three companions; on the lower level, representing the earthly sphere, Peter, James and John are portrayed in various states of shock and terror, with only Peter just beginning to dare to kneel up and behold what is taking place. The figure of Jesus is suspended in a circular *mandorla*, which surrounds his whole body like a halo, and which is a symbolic convention in icon painting for representing the glory of God. Strong and penetrating rays of 'uncreated light' emanate from the figure of Christ, to touch all parts of the painting, and draw us, the viewer, in, carrying us also 'up the mountain' to fix our gaze on God and to be transformed by his beauty and light.[10]

MORALITY OR MYSTERY?

The emphasis given to the Transfiguration in the Eastern Church focuses on its significance as the cosmic revelation of the Son's glory to all believers (not just the three disciples who were present), the other occasion for such a revelation being the Resurrection itself. As Michael Ramsey puts it, 'While some Western expositors have asked what moral and practical lessons are to be learnt from the event, the East has often been content simply to rejoice in the glory which Mount Tabor sheds upon Christ, the Christians and all creation.'[11] Indeed, Ramsey's words reflect something of the contrast of approach to the Transfiguration between East and West, and may begin to suggest why the West has struggled with it, especially during the last millennium. Put in a nutshell (and generalising enormously), the Western tendency has been to dismiss anything that pertains to 'the mystical', whereas the Eastern Church has delighted in 'the mystical' as one of the central tenets of the Orthodox faith.[12] In the West, the Transfiguration has been seen to be something that must be *explained*, whereas in the East it has been something to be *experienced*.

Stephen Barton, in a recent article,[13] helpfully identifies several factors that have led to a reticence in the Western tradition in relation to the Transfiguration. Amongst them, he points to the effect of the Reformation in its 'narrowing' of an authentic canon of Christian truth to Scripture and conscience, leaving little, if any room for 'experience'; secondly, he points to the rationalism of the Enlightenment, which demanded that all things may be understood by the human mind; thirdly, he suggests that the nineteenth and twentieth centuries have each contributed further to this modernist approach to theological truth, whereby what cannot be understood rationally must be thought of as 'myth', and where epistemological theory becomes the arbiter of truth. If one adds to this list of factors the roots of Western theology in the Scholasticism of Aquinas and the overwhelming preoccupation of the last one hundred years with the search for the historical Jesus, it is not surprising that anything which smacks of the mystical (such as the Transfiguration) should have been relegated to the shadows of theological and liturgical consciousness!

Against such a background, a variety of suggestions have been offered to 'explain' the Transfiguration. Boobyer, in his seminal work, *St Mark and the Transfiguration Story*,[14] offers several possibilities, built on by Ramsey some years later.[15] Amongst these is the suggestion that the Transfiguration story is a piece of symbolic writing, incorporated into the Gospel narrative as a means of substantiating the Jewish eschatological hope that Jesus was the Messiah and the inaugurator of the New Age.[16] Another idea is that the Transfiguration did not actually *happen*, but that it should be treated in psychological terms as a 'historical experience of a visionary nature' (G. H. Boobyer), not unlike those attributed to St Francis of Assisi, Teresa of Avila and Julian of Norwich, amongst others. Ramsey, however, is unimpressed by this suggestion – not least because it is unlikely that three disciples should share the *same* vision (although Harnack suggests that it was Peter's vision and the others were added later to give it strength).[17]

Perhaps the most popular 'explanation' of the Transfiguration during the early and mid-twentieth century was that it was originally a Resurrection story,[18] transferred back into the Gospel narrative, supposedly as a means of 'allowing' the disciples to 'understand' the Resurrection when it occurred. Ramsey, however, sees no justification for this suggestion (as neither do more recent scholars), and finds particular difficulties in accounting for the presence of Moses and Elijah in such an interpretation. Unlike most of his contemporaries, however, he does concede that the Transfiguration may be understood in terms of Christian mysticism (cf. the Orthodox approach outlined above), and cites Evelyn Underhill as one of the main proponents of this theory.[19]

This very brief outline of the chasm between the Eastern and Western approaches to the Transfiguration may begin to give us some idea as to why (in the West) it has been largely a 'forgotten feast'. It has defied rational explanation and has therefore tended to be rejected or at least ignored. Visions of light and supernatural experiences have not been considered 'normal' and those who experience them have often come under suspicion. Indeed, despite the fact that there is increasing evidence that such 'spiritual experience' is being taken more seriously, it is considered simply as *personal experience* in a post-modern world, where each is free to express and believe what they choose and there is no longer any globally accepted meta-narrative to which experience may be related. In such a world, there could be a million transfigurations, each as 'valid' as any other, but of no significance for all.

Little wonder, then, that so little has been written in recent years about the Transfiguration. It is time to look again and to explore not only the biblical texts and the themes which emerge from them, but also to engage with what does not 'make sense' in a rational way, and to allow the Spirit of God – present on Mount Tabor and present here and now – to enlighten not only our minds but our hearts also, as we take time to encounter afresh this vision of God in Jesus Christ.

Chapter 3

◆

THROUGH THE EYES OF PETER

ONE PERSON FOR WHOM the Transfiguration was clearly of deep significance was the apostle Peter, and we turn now to look at the event, as it were, 'through Peter's eyes', as we explore the accounts in the Synoptic Gospels and 2 Peter. It must be said that here is not the place for close exegetical study. That task has been done already, and continues to form the work of much finer scholars than ourselves; suffice it here to outline the main emphases of the Transfiguration in each of the Synoptic Gospels, and to identify particular similarities, differences and features as they emerge through our study of Peter.

The earliest account of the Transfiguration is that which appears in Mark chapter 9. Peter is widely regarded as the key witness and source for the Marcan narrative as a whole, and clearly his presence as only one of three witnesses to the event of the Transfiguration would suggest that Marcan/Petrine material is likely to have contributed to the Matthean and Lukan accounts also. Only those who had been present on the mountain could have known what was said, who was there and what the experience was like. Thus, although each Gospel writer moulds the Transfiguration material to fit within the particular shape and thrust of his Gospel as a whole, the core material is common to all.

So what are the particular emphases of each Transfiguration account?[1] Mark's key concern (Mark 9:2–8ff) is to prove that Jesus is, indeed, the Messiah of God to a Christian community that is becoming increasingly pressurised and unpopular. The glory of God revealed on the mountain demonstrates not only Jesus' divinity, but also foreshadows the end time – the Parousia – when Christ will be revealed in glory to the whole earth.[2] This revelation, in time, of the glory of eternity was offered as an encouragement to faithful discipleship, not only for Peter, James and John, but also for the suffering and persecuted Christian community for whom Mark was writing.

Matthew's account of the Transfiguration (17:1–8) is heavily dependent upon Mark. He too is keen to underline the fact that Jesus is the Messiah, the fulfilment of Jewish hopes, in whom the glory of God, partially revealed to the people of Israel, is now finally and completely made known in the person of Jesus Christ. There is a distinctly 'Jewish' flavour about Matthew's account, with his reference to 'the shining face of Jesus' (cf. Moses in Exodus 34:9ff) and the prominence of the overshadowing cloud, with its echoes of the Exodus and anticipation of the Second Coming. For Matthew especially, the presence of God is past, present and future.

In Luke, the Transfiguration has a somewhat different 'feel' to the other two Synoptic Gospels. The whole episode takes place in the context of prayer, and it is in *this* context that God's glory is revealed. The 'conversation' with Moses and Elijah (upon which Peter, James and John are allowed to eavesdrop) is specifically focused upon Jesus' impending journey to Jerusalem and the suffering he will endure. Moreover the fact that the three disciples are 'weighed down with sleep' (v. 32) is reminiscent of a similar scene in Gethsemane (Luke 22:35) and the links with impending suffering are obvious.

Having offered, as background, a 'flavour' of the story of the Transfiguration in each of the Synoptic Gospels, it is time to attempt to look at the event through Peter's eyes. As we do so, five key themes will begin to emerge and will form the backbone of this book as we explore the significance of the Transfiguration for today.

1. KNOWING CHRIST

About a week before the Transfiguration, Peter had made the most astounding statement of his life. On the way to Caesarea Philippi, Jesus had asked his disciples, 'Who do people say that I am?' and Peter had made the unambiguous reply, 'You are the Messiah.'[3] This revelation to those few disciples who were with him was to remain secret from the crowds until the right time, but the process of working through its implications was begun immediately. At Caesarea Philippi, Peter had been given unique insight into who Jesus was; yet within moments, as Jesus begins to talk openly (for the second time) about his coming suffering, death and resurrection, Peter shows himself to be 'blind' again, rebuking Jesus for speaking in this way. The one whom he had just identified as Messiah was apparently not known to him at all: insight gave way not even to 'sight', but to blindness, and what followed was some straightforward teaching about the cost of discipleship and the future glory of the Son of Man.[4]

Peter has, therefore, been travelling with Jesus for about a week, time enough to ponder on both who he is and what he has said – especially his words, 'Truly I tell you, there are some standing here who will not taste death until they see that the kingdom of God has come with power' (Mark 9:1; cf. Matt. 16:28; Luke 9:27). Perhaps he thought he knew Jesus well, particularly since he and James and John – the inner circle of Jesus' disciples – were sometimes called away from the rest to accompany him. So it may have come as no surprise to be invited to go with him up the mountain. What did surprise him, however, was the nature of the experience which followed, for he witnessed, in symbolic form, confirmation of the truth he had expressed a week earlier and saw, with his own eyes, the glory of the Messiah made known in the person of Jesus. As Rob Marshall comments:

> The Transfiguration is . . . a symbolic vision of Peter's confession of faith . . . Jesus is the Son of God, the glorious Messiah: Peter confesses him as such and then sees the reality of this for himself.[5]

For Peter, 'knowing Christ' was not a static state but a dynamic one, for the one who 'knew' him at Caesarea Philippi failed immediately to understand what was to follow. Similarly, the one who 'knew' him on the mountain would, within a very short time, deny that he was with him.[6] His knowledge of Christ (in the sense of his relationship *with* Christ) was to 'rise and fall', to 'ebb and flow'. His human frailty and sinfulness so frequently 'got in the way', causing him to doubt that about which he was once certain and leading him to 'forget' that which he once knew. Yet the experience of the Transfiguration was to remain with Peter for the rest of his earthly life;[7] it was to be 'folded in' and to become part of the 'bedrock' of his faith.

For us, like Peter, 'knowing Christ' is about more than mere *recognition*, and it is not something that we achieve once and for all. It is a living discovery where blindness gives way to sight and insight and back again, where (unlike his knowledge of *us*) we can never take our knowledge of him for granted, and where we will not know Christ fully until we see him 'face to face'. We too are frail, sinful and forgetful, and yet, like Peter, our many 'little transfigurations' may become part of the 'bedrock' of *our* faith, encounters through which we see and know Christ and our world in new and life-changing ways.

2. WORSHIP AND FEAR

When Peter cried out, 'Lord, it is good for us to be here!' it was, more than anything, an exclamation of joy. It was an affirmation (on behalf of James and John also) that to be in the presence of the glory of God in Christ was wonderful and awe-full at one and the same time. Echoes of Isaiah 6 and Revelation 1 come immediately to mind. Never one to be lost for words, Peter suggests, somewhat bizarrely, the construction of three booths to 'contain' Moses and Elijah and Jesus (the significance of which we shall explore shortly). Fundamentally, he is overwhelmed by the presence of God and there is only one response – to fall at his feet in worship.

So how was the presence of God made known? Three phenomena are mentioned in the Gospels: a dazzling light, the cloud and the voice, together with the fact that the episode took place 'on a high mountain'. This latter detail is significant. To the Jewish mind, high mountains are places of revelation: Moses and Elijah each meet with God on a mountain;[8] Jesus chooses to pray on the mountain[9] and is even tempted by the devil on a mountain.[10] In addition, Jesus ascended from a mountain[11] and rabbinic literature cited a mountain as the expected location for the Second Coming.[12] Peter would have been aware that the invitation to climb a mountain with Jesus would, in all likelihood, have resulted in something special taking place.

Nevertheless, the shock of what happened should not be underestimated. The combination of dazzling light, the cloud and the voice must have been terrifying for the three disciples. Powerful light emanated from the person of Jesus himself and his clothes became a dazzling white.[13] In Mark and Matthew, we are told that he was 'transfigured before them'. (It is worth pointing out at this stage that Luke's Gospel does not speak of the 'transfiguration' of Christ – rather, he says that 'as he was praying, *the appearance of his countenance was altered*'.[14] This apparent reticence to use the Greek verb μεταμορφοομαι (*metamorphoomai*) is explained by the fact that he was writing to a primarily Gentile audience, who may have been inclined to associate the event, unhelpfully, with the 'metamorphosis' of heathen gods. Mark and Matthew, by contrast, do employ the term – *meta* implying 'change' and *morphe* meaning 'form'.[15] The verb occurs in only two other places in the New Testament: Romans 12:2, 'Be transformed by the renewing of your minds', and 2 Corinthians 3:18, 'And all of us . . . are being transformed into the same image' – the present continuous tense implying a *process* of transformation rather than the passive voice which is used to describe the 'one-off' event of the Transfiguration of Jesus Christ.) The change of appearance of Jesus' face is also noted by Matthew (17:2) – 'his face shone like the sun' – reminiscent of the reflected glory of Moses' face in Exodus 34:29ff. What is certain is that Peter, James and John were confronted with an unearthly brightness as they caught a glimpse of this divine light.

As if that was not enough, there is also the cloud and the voice. Again, like the 'mountain', both phenomena are rooted in the Old Testament[16] and in Jewish apocalyptic. The *shekinah* cloud is a symbol of revelation in the present as well as of future glory – a vehicle God uses and through which he speaks – so linking the Transfiguration with both the Ascension and the Second Coming.[17] The voice affirms the divine presence, revealing to all who are present both the relationship between Father and Son and the divine authority with which Jesus speaks and acts. Little wonder that Peter, James and John fall to the ground, terrified!

Yet it is a fear which is not altogether negative, for, in the context of worship (which, in essence, is what this is), Peter's and his friends' fear is more about awe, reverence and respect than it is about terror and alarm. This distinction between what is basically a Jewish and a Greek understanding of the word φοβος (*phobos*) is important here – for, in the *Jewish* understanding, fear is matched by God's grace, and Peter, in all his feeble humanity, can face this powerful vision of the glory of God, aware that he is accepted and loved.

For us, Peter's experience on the mountain may raise many questions. For example, how often do we obey his call to 'come apart' and go to the mountain with Jesus? What do we expect to happen? Who do we expect to see? And how do we respond to those moments when we catch a glimpse of the glory of God in Jesus Christ – with reverence or with fear or both? The Transfiguration opens up a wealth of exploration concerning our worship and our prayer, both in terms of expectation and experience; if nothing else, it surely convicts us of the shallowness of the encounter and the feeble dullness of much that we offer.

3. TIME AND EXPERIENCE

One of the more unusual elements of the Transfiguration story is the presence of Moses and Elijah on the mountain with Jesus, and Peter's bizarre suggestion, 'If you wish, I will make three dwellings here, one for you, one for Moses and one for Elijah' (Matt. 17:4). What *did* Peter mean? Was this simply the ridiculous babbling of a man suffering from shock, or was there some significance in what he was saying? And why were Moses and Elijah present in the first place?

When we begin to answer those questions, it becomes clear that, for Peter and his contemporaries, a vision of Jesus with Moses and Elijah was not so odd as it might seem to us. Peter and his fellow disciples were living in an age of great expectation. The Jewish people were full of anticipation that Messiah would come, and Elijah the prophet was always closely associated with that coming – hence the conversation about John the Baptist as 'Elijah' as they were coming down from the mountain.[18] By contrast, Moses would have epitomised the Torah for Peter and his companions – Moses was the giver of the Law that had, for so long, symbolised the covenant relationship of God with his people Israel. A vision of Jesus with Moses and Elijah would have suggested to Peter both that Jesus was the natural fulfiller of all that had been given in the Torah (a link to the past), and also that, revealed in his present glory, Jesus was the one who was to come, the

Messiah of God (a link to the future). In short, Jesus is presented as one who encompasses time and eternity, to whom the two key figures of the Jewish faith bear witness.

In the light of this, Peter's suggestion to build three dwellings begins to make some sense. The dwellings (or 'booths') relate to the Feast of Tabernacles – a 'harvest festival' of the Jewish people.[19] It is a festival which looks both backwards and forwards: backwards to the wilderness wanderings of the people of Israel; forwards to the time when all nations shall worship with Israel, and God will 'tabernacle' with his people. As was so often the case, Peter was 'on the right track' when he made his comment about building the dwellings, but didn't quite get it right – for the Transfiguration was a visual *anticipation* of the Second Coming, but not the *actual* Second Coming. It was not yet time for the 'dwellings' to be inhabited.

It is not surprising, therefore, that the early Church latched on to Peter and his companions' account of the Transfiguration as a key source of encouragement as they awaited the Parousia, the final revelation of Christ – especially as they suffered persecution and mocking from those around them, who said it would never happen! In this way, three people's experience (and, in particular, their experience as recorded by Peter) was to become a rich resource for the whole Church. An event which may not have been fully understood when it happened, and which took place 'in time', was to transcend time, and to take on meaning *beyond itself* not only for those who experienced it, but for those with whom the story was shared.

For Peter, this is illustrated in 2 Peter 1:15–18. It is almost certain that Peter himself did not write this letter.[20] Yet the fact that it is presented as a kind of 'testament' – the last words of a dying man (see v. 15) – lends weight to the message it contains. Whoever the author might be, it is clear that the experience of the Transfiguration continued to hold enormous impact for Peter himself throughout his life, and was seen as a profound marker of his apostolic witness.

For us, significant experiences do not always make sense. We can find ourselves saying and doing things which seem illogical at the time. Sometimes, it can seem almost impossible to get beyond reliving the event itself. Peter's experience on the mountain encourages us to recognise that particular events can speak to past, present and future. Time itself can be transfigured and what seemed incomprehensible can become a source of hope and encouragement not only for ourselves but for many others also. The Transfiguration has much to teach us about how we value and understand experience, and how it might be used for the good of all.

4. SUFFERING

So far, as we have looked at the Transfiguration 'through Peter's eyes', we have concentrated on his awareness of the glory of God demonstrated in dazzling light and cloud and voice on the mountain. Peter's response has been one of worship and reverence and awe, but also one of only partial comprehension and the utterance of strange words.

In Luke's Gospel another strand emerges. We read, 'Suddenly they saw two men, Moses and Elijah, talking to him. They appeared in glory and were speaking of his departure,[21] which he was about to accomplish at Jerusalem. Now Peter and his companions were weighed down with sleep' (Luke 9:30–32). Here, Peter is not open-mouthed in awe and expectation, but almost struck unconscious, unable to take in what is happening. Luke's words, 'they were speaking of [Jesus'] departure, which he was about to accomplish at Jerusalem', point to the Passion and the fact that glory is to be revealed as much through the cross as through incarnation, resurrection and exaltation. In a tacit echo of the conversation that followed Peter's confession at Caesarea Philippi, and foreshadowing the scene in the Garden, Peter is depicted as shunning and trying to avoid the truth that suffering must accompany glory. He failed to understand. It is only later, as he encourages others who are suffering, that he is able to articulate (in word and action) the truth which he had witnessed on the mountain, describing himself as 'a witness of the sufferings of Christ, as well as one who shares in the glory to be revealed' (1 Pet. 5:1).

Peter had to learn that the way of glory was the way of the Cross. He found it extraordinarily hard to accept, for it went against all his preconceptions of what God is like. For him, the experience of the Transfiguration was to be both a challenge and an anchor as he walked the tightrope of suffering and hope, and encouraged others to do the same. For us, as for many people of vision[22] over the ages, the Transfiguration may help us to hold glory and suffering together as we too, in many and various ways, are called to come down from the mountain and face our own 'Jerusalem'.

5. OBEDIENCE AND DISCIPLESHIP

More than anything, it is hearing the voice of God through the cloud which has an impact upon Peter. He had witnessed strange happenings before – healings, exorcisms, miraculous feeding of great crowds, the stilling of the waters at Jesus' command – but nothing as extraordinary as this. On the mountain of Transfiguration, he and his companions hear the words of God, 'This is my Son, the beloved;[23] listen to him!' (Mark 9:7). Identification and command come together. At his Baptism in the Jordan, the voice from heaven speaks primarily to Jesus himself; it is an affirmation of who he is at the beginning of his earthly ministry. In the Transfiguration, the voice is heard by *all* who are present – a declaration and proclamation of the Beloved Son of God, his 'Chosen One' (Luke 9:35), and the command which accompanies it is a call to obedient discipleship.

Peter is told to 'Listen to him'. The weight of the command

lies in its context, for to some extent, Peter has already been 'listening to him' – although there is clearly much that he has failed to understand. Yet when the command is heard at the same time as the glory is revealed, it carries with it an intensity and expectation which is irresistible. The call to discipleship could not have been spoken more clearly, and it came at a point when things were going to become even tougher for Jesus and his followers. Not that Peter's discipleship would be unwavering; far from it! But the 'Listen to him!' of the Transfiguration must have resonated through his life, in the same way as the 'Follow me!' of his call[24] (and re-call[25]) must have done – and particularly at times of difficulty and temptation.

For us, the Transfiguration focuses both the vision of the glory of God in Christ, the response to which is worship, and also the command to listen to the words of Christ, the response to which is obedient discipleship. You cannot have one without the other – a truth made known most completely in the person of Jesus Christ himself. As Stephen C. Barton comments:

> The transfiguration is an invitation to share in the life of God revealed in the Son of God and mediated by the Spirit of God, by learning obedience in the good company of those who follow him ... Like Christ, glory comes from bearing and embodying faithful, passionate witness to the will of God.[26]

Looking at the Transfiguration through the eyes of Peter has allowed us to identify the key elements of this event as portrayed in the Synoptic Gospels, and also to begin to uncover what it may have to say to us in our daily living. The themes of Knowing Christ, Worship and Fear, Time and Experience, Suffering, and Obedience and Discipleship are all present in this extraordinary story. It is a rich and deep soil in which to dig – a soil that becomes even more fruitful when we turn to the Gospel of John.

Chapter 4

◆

I HAVE
SEEN THE LORD

IN THIS CHAPTER WE EXPLORE the Transfiguration theme in John's Gospel, knowing that John sees the Transfiguration (and much else) in a different way to the Synoptic Gospels. He sees it as an ongoing event – something which permeates the life and ministry of Jesus. For John it is clear that Jesus reveals the glory of God throughout his life, death, resurrection and ascension, and through his Spirit-filled disciples. Faith enables those who believe to have sight accompanied sometimes by insight, and for them glory may be revealed through the ordinary events of life with Jesus. The glory is revealed particularly in the 'signs' and focused in the person of Jesus through the 'I AM' sayings.

In Luke's Gospel the voice from heaven at the Transfiguration says, 'This is my Son, my Chosen; listen to him.' In John's Gospel we may hear the same voice drawing us to identify Jesus as God's Son (the use of the 'I AM' sayings), as God's chosen one (who shares the name and nature of God) and as the one to whom we should attend. In John's Gospel, however, the emphasis is on 'seeing'. We are invited, especially by the 'signs', to see the glory of God in Jesus, and to be transformed ourselves by that sight. These, then, are our themes as we explore this Gospel – the 'I AM' sayings, the signs, how sight gives way to insight, and the name and nature of God.

'I AM'

If the presence of Moses and Elijah in the synoptic accounts of the Transfiguration revealed Jesus both as a link with the past as well as hope for the future, then in John's Gospel the use of the words 'I AM' and the 'I AM' sayings suggest the same embrace of time and eternity. In particular, in discussion with the Jews at the Feast of Tabernacles Jesus makes the astounding statement, 'Your ancestor Abraham rejoiced that he would see my day; he saw it and was glad . . . Very truly I tell you, before Abraham was I am.'[1] His claim to bear the name of God – this divine name caught in the Greek words *ego eimi* – was sufficient for the Jews to 'pick up stones to throw at him'. Clearly, this use of words was seen to be a claim to be divine and was sufficient to warrant the response due to one guilty of blasphemy – one whom 'the whole congregation shall stone'.[2]

Elsewhere too in the Gospel it is clear that Jesus' use of 'I AM' is seen as a revelation of the divine. For example, in John's account of the arrest, Jesus says, 'I am he', the response of his captors being to step back and fall to the ground.[3] When they respond to his question, 'Who are you looking for?' the second time, he again says, 'I am', and they arrest him. In another incident in John 6 Jesus is found walking on water and he says to the disciples, 'Do not be afraid, I am (he).' This incident echoes many in the Old Testament where divine revelation is often accompanied with the command. 'Do not be afraid.'[4]

Jesus' use of the words 'I AM' does not, however, always mean that revelation is the only level of meaning. A number of interpretations are sometimes possible. Sometimes the use of 'I AM' is not precise. In John 13:19, for example, Jesus says, 'you may believe that I am (he),' but he does not indicate who they are to believe he is. At other times the context makes the use of the words clearer. In John 6, when Jesus walks on water, it is almost as though 'I AM' is saying, 'It's me, your friend.' In a third and more direct way Jesus uses 'I AM' to offer images of his nature[5] – the bread of life, the light of the world, the gate for the sheep, the good shepherd, the resurrection and the life, the way, the truth and the life, and the vine.

These sayings reveal clearly that Jesus' self-understanding is involved in these images. We cannot therefore overestimate what the words 'I AM' (Greek *ego eimi*) convey. In 2 Isaiah, for example, and especially in the Septuagint version, the words *ego eimi* refer clearly to God's name – 'I, I am he.'[6] Jesus is fully aware and articulate about his relationship to the Father when he uses these words. He is echoing the (to us) unheard voice which says, 'This is my Son.'

THE 'SIGNS'

In the introduction to this chapter we said that the emphasis on 'seeing' in John's Gospel is another way of attracting our attention to the figure, words and deeds of Jesus. It is not surprising that John emphasises sight. In fact, to sight he marries insight. In his Gospel we are able to ponder the life of Jesus at many different levels. John intends too that we not only see but believe. It has been said that 'Words inform, relationships transform.'[7] John's intention is not just to convey words which inform us but to enable us to encounter the 'Word made flesh' who will, *by his very being*, lead us to the transformation of our lives. Jesus is not replacing what has gone before. He is instead transforming it and building upon it 'grace upon grace'.[8] The signs may helpfully be seen in this light.

In the Synoptic accounts of the Transfiguration Moses witnesses, by his presence, to what had gone before. In John's Gospel Moses seems to stand beside Jesus throughout the

Gospel and attest to the glory revealed in Christ. In the 'signs' themselves we may see a parallel to the 'signs' that Moses performed as God's people escaped from Egypt (dividing the water, the provision of manna etc.). These are great 'works' of God revealing his will for his people. In both the Old Testament and in John's Gospel such works are often accompanied by words which interpret them. So, in John 6, for example, there is a discourse after the feeding of the five thousand.[9] R. E. Brown makes the point that the 'Word reminds us that the value of the miracle is not in its form but in its content; the miraculous work reminds us that the word is not empty, but an active, energetic word designed to change the world'[10] (his italics).

Jesus himself claims that Moses is his witness when he says, 'your accuser is Moses . . . if you believed Moses, you would believe me for he wrote about me', and John sees Jesus as going further than Moses: 'law indeed was given through Moses; grace and truth came through Jesus Christ.'[11] The signs, then, are clearly intended to both reveal the glory of God and evoke belief – John's intention for his whole understanding of the Gospel message.[12]

The seven signs[13] invite the onlookers and readers of the Gospel to see beyond the events and recognise who Jesus is – they invite us to look at Jesus' face and, seeing beyond it, experience the glory of the Father.[14] Nothing can be taken at face value. All that Jesus is and does is indicative of the Father.[15] In *being* the Father's Son and *doing* the Father's work, Jesus is not just performing works of power. He is seeking to evoke faith. The response of those who see and hear is therefore crucial.[16]

R. E. Brown identifies four responses of faith which are closely paralleled by reactions to these signs. They relate to our use of 'sight and insight'.[17] The first two reactions are the reactions of sight:

(a) The reactions of those who refuse to see the signs

with any faith . . . their wilful blindness can only be explained by the lack of faith predicted in the Old Testament.[18]

(b) The reactions of those who see the signs as wonders and believe in Jesus as a wonder-worker sent by God . . . it is not sufficient to be impressed by the miracles as wonders wrought by the power of God; they must also be seen as a revelation of who Jesus is, and his oneness with the Father.[19]

Beyond these reactions are the reactions of insight:

(c) The reaction of those who see the true significance of the signs, and thus come to believe in Jesus and to know who he is and his relationship to the Father . . . It is this understanding of a sign that enables the believer to see that Jesus is the manifestation of God's glory.[20]

(d) The reaction of those who believe in Jesus even without seeing signs.[21]

In revealing the glory of God the signs are therefore an invitation to know Jesus as the one sent by the Father – in the same way that the Transfiguration was seen in Chapter 3 to be about knowing Christ. They involve transformation, but the most important element of that transformation is the ability to *see*, *know* and *be transformed* by Christ. So, in the same way that the Book of Deuteronomy says, 'Never since has there arisen a prophet like Moses, whom the Lord knew face to face. He was unequalled for all the signs and wonders that the Lord sent him to perform . . .', St John says, 'Now Jesus did many other signs in the presence of his disciples that are not written in this book. But these are written *so that you may come to believe* . . . '[22]

SIGHT AND INSIGHT

One of the tragedies of both Old and New Testament is the failure of people to move on from sight to belief.[23] In chapter 12 of his Gospel John explains this unbelief by reference to Isaiah 53:1 and 6:10 – two favourite passage for this purpose. More than sight, therefore, is needed, and belief happens when sight gives way to insight. For those with insight the glory of God is revealed in the whole of Jesus' life, death and resurrection. As we read John's Gospel, it is almost as if the transfigured Christ stands before us. John invites us to open our eyes and see. And yet he knows that it is not always possible for us to see. As Thérèse of Lisieux says, the face of Christ both conceals and reveals. Without insight it is simply another face. Insight is the result of faith, grace and the ability to interpret.

In his encounters with people, Jesus uses the ordinary to reveal the extraordinary. The whole of life becomes sacramental in the sense that it reveals signs of the dimension of the holy, which in fact is always present but not always recognised. So transfiguration becomes a living experience and not a one-off event.

One incident highlights this clearly. In John 4 Jesus meets the Samaritan woman. In this encounter Jesus' thirst is both physical and spiritual. He longs for a response of faith. As he talks to the woman she sees beyond face value and is drawn by his understanding and love. Gradually her own faith is kindled and she interprets the meeting in the light of her own faith and its expectations of a Messiah.[24] Only grace enables her to do this – the grace of his presence. Sight and insight are interwoven, and Jesus reveals himself in a moment of transfiguration glory – 'I am he', *'ego eimi'*. Again we are not told whether or not her life was changed beyond her immediate surprise and wonder. It is hard to imagine, however, that life would ever be the same again, and Jesus

34

indicates to her that she will come to have this deeper insight, so that she may come to worship in spirit and in truth.

In this revelation of himself Jesus, as we noted earlier in this chapter, is drawing attention not to himself but to the Father whom she will worship.[25] His own authority comes only from the Father – whose name and nature he shares.

THE NAME AND NATURE OF GOD

Speaking of the importance of the name in Jewish understanding, D. S. Russell writes:

> The name is no mere appellation; it is, so to speak, an 'extension' of the man's personality and indicates his essential being, his life, his very self. Thus to honour a man's name or the name of God is to honour the one who bears it; to blot out one's name is to annihilate the man himself and all that he represents. So closely associated are the ideas of 'character' and 'name' that a change in character or circumstance often involves a change in name. But a man's name is not confined simply to himself; it can be shared with others or inherited with them.[26]

This throws considerable light on the significance of the 'name' in John's Gospel, where the living God has given himself in sending a Son into whose hands he has placed all things.[27]

Jesus says that he has come in the Father's name,[28] he acts in the Father's name,[29] those who believe in his name have the right to become children of God but those who reject stand condemned,[30] the Spirit would be sent in his name and those who believed could pray and act in this name.[31] Indeed, those who follow him will suffer his rejection because of the name but will also know God's protection.[32] In his name the readers of the Gospel may have life.

For other writers the name which Jesus is given which is

above other names is 'Lord', but the name for John is perhaps
the 'I AM'. It is the name that the Father shares with the Son
rather than the name which disciples will give him. It is the
name of sonship which will be shared with those who believe –
those who have the right to be called 'children of God',[33] who
were born 'of God'.

Pedersen points out that 'The soul in its entirety, with all
its blessing and honour finds expression in the name. To know
the name of a man is to know his essence.'[34] And the essence
is love. Jesus has no doubt that the very being of God is love.
The Father loves the Son[35] and loves the world. In the glory
of the Father the Son has known that love since before the
foundation of the world.[36]

The revelation of Jesus is not only of the glory of God but
of the very nature of God – love. If there is to be transfiguration, it will be of those who believe, who discover that they
are loved and who reach out with that love to others. Here is
the foundation on which any response to Jesus may be
made, the means by which our own discipleship is to be lived
out. The challenge is not so much about understanding but
about experiencing and living . . . and so the invitation, 'Come
and see.'[37]

When Jesus gives his new commandment he makes two
startling claims – that he loves us and that we can love each
other with that same love. We can do that only insofar as we
stay united with him as he is united with the Father. We are
to obey his command as he obeys the Father's command – in
the knowledge of and as a response to love. This changes our
way of seeing how 'glory revealed' is to be lived out and
draws us to reflect again on those same themes which
emerged from our study of the Synoptic Gospels:

1. Knowing Christ

Jesus says simply, 'This is eternal life, that they may know
you, the only true God, and Jesus Christ whom you have

sent.'[38] Knowledge of Jesus and so of the Father is central to John's Gospel. Throughout it there is a tension between knowing and not knowing – many simply do not know who Jesus is, though they claim some knowledge about him (e.g. about his parentage).[39]

The contrast is clear between the way that Jesus knows people[40] and the way that they do not truly know him nor the Father.[41] What marks out Jesus' disciples is that they are the ones who are both known by and who come to know Jesus, the Father *and* the Spirit.[42] This knowledge is only possible by mutual indwelling. It is a gift by which glory is given to the Father, but also to the Son and to those who believe. When fulfilment comes, 'you will know that I am in the Father and you in me, and I in you.'[43]

Indeed, without pushing the point too far, we may see some parallels between 'knowledge' and 'transition'. For example, in the Synoptic accounts, the events at Caesarea Philippi,[44] where Peter identifies Jesus as the Messiah of God, are followed by the Transfiguration and then by Jesus' 'setting his face to Jerusalem'.[45] In John's account there are similar moments. In John 12 the Greeks who come to see Jesus provoke another 'setting of his face' (though John does not use those words), and Jesus becomes the seed that must fall into the ground.[46] Later, having shared much with his disciples, they come to understand that 'he knows all things' and 'truly comes from God'. Then Jesus sets his face again to the events of his passion, death, resurrection and ascension (the 'hour' of John 16:32). Knowledge initiates action.

After the resurrection another incident between Jesus and Peter highlights this theme. Peter recognises that 'Jesus knows all things'[47] and in that understanding he is committed to a discipleship he can scarcely ever have imagined. In the encounter with Thomas too we are drawn into this obedience and discipleship – we who have not seen and yet believe.[48]

What is also clear in these two encounters is Jesus' deep and compassionate knowledge of Peter and Thomas. To know and be known is to be living in the breath of that Spirit which blows where it wills.[49] It is to be empowered by that Spirit to come to deeper knowledge.[50]

There is, then, for those who believe, a double knowledge – knowing and being known. For those who cannot see and yet believe, the gift of the Holy Spirit is clearly essential to guide us into all truth and to the deepening of this knowledge.

2. *Worship and fear*

If the prologue of John's Gospel is read prayerfully, then it inculcates worship, awe and adoration:

> In the beginning was the Word, and the Word was with God, and the Word was God. He was in the beginning with God. All things came into being through him, and without him not one thing came into being. What has come into being in him was life, and the life was the light of all people. The light shines in the darkness, but the darkness did not overcome it . . .
>
> And the Word became flesh and lived among us and we have seen his glory, the glory as of a Father's only son, full of grace and truth . . . From his fullness we have all received grace upon grace. The law indeed was given through Moses; grace and truth came through Jesus Christ. No one has ever seen God. It is God the only Son, who is close to the Father's heart, who has made him known.

Worship, then, is implied throughout John's Gospel. Jesus wants people not to fall at his feet (though the blind man worships him and Mary kneels before him)[51] but to know the Father and live his truth. Worship is about living in love. There is much awe and respect but little fear, in the sense of terror. St John sees God as a love which casts out fear.[52] So St John reveals Christ, even in the Passion, to be at one with the Father. There is in Gethsemane little anguish, from the Cross

no cry of despair. Instead Jesus reveals an attitude of love as
he binds his mother to the beloved disciple. Here is a Jesus
who invites worship, who, though fully and unquestionably
human, reveals what it means to worship the Father in spirit
and in truth. For those who have insight, he is acclaimed
'Lord and God'.

3. *Time and experience*

For John the figure of Jesus was more than the figure of a man.
Jesus, though truly Word made flesh, was clearly identified in
time as a historical figure who revealed an authoritative
presence among his people. But he was also the one loved
before the foundation of the world and who had an existence
with the Father. He goes beyond definitions of time but also
enters time in intensity and reality.

John's use of the word 'glory' is enough to make this clear.
If in the Old Testament the glory of God was the means by
which a normally invisible God made his presence known,[53]
it was also the means by which mighty acts were performed
(e.g. manna in Exodus 16 and water in Exodus 17). John
embraces both understandings. Jesus reveals the glory of God
in order to manifest his presence but also, in the signs, to
perform the works of God. R. E. Brown writes: 'It is true
that John does not describe the Transfiguration which for the
synoptic is really the only manifestation of glory among
the public ministry (Luke 9:32). Yet John does stress that the
divine doxa shone through Jesus' miraculous signs (2:11;
11:40; 17:4).'[54]

St John understands that the glory was present and active
in the 'Word made flesh'. He also recognises that the glory is
uniquely revealed through the passion, death and resurrection
of Jesus. Even these events point to a final unique revelation
of glory.

4. *Suffering*

That glory is not distinct from suffering nor limited by it. Indeed, glory is revealed in humility. The one who is Master washes his disciples' feet and, as he will later lay aside his life, so then he lays aside his clothes. Somehow the glory of Christ – the glory he has only because he seeks to glorify the Father – holds together union with God and going the furthest distance and accepting death. Jesus himself recognises this as he approaches his Passion and talks of the seed that must die.[55] Glory for the disciples as well as for Jesus comes from serving the Father, sharing the name,[56] serving Christ and serving each other.

Service, of necessity, implies humility – earthiness – and earthiness involves suffering. God's glory takes us to the heart of his creation and is not in any way removed from it. Yet we no longer 'belong' to the world, we are not held by the world. We belong to God and should not be surprised if the world (that which rejects God) hates us.

For Peter especially, the connection between suffering and glory, discipleship and cross, is made explicit. His love for Christ implies a share in loving the sheep for which Jesus has laid down his life, but it will also involve his own suffering as he glorifies the Father:

> 'You will stretch out your hands, and someone will fasten a belt around you and take you where you do not wish to go.' (He said this to indicate the kind of death by which he would glorify God.) After this he said, 'Follow me.'[57]

5. *Obedience and discipleship*

John draws us to a vision of love in which discipleship and obedience are made possible. As Ramsey says, 'There can be no imitation of Christ until first there has been the receiving of the judgement and the love which the passion brings.'[58] We are to be empowered by that love for which Jesus prays to the Father,[59] 'so that the love with which you have loved me may be in them and I in them.' The love which has sustained Christ's ministry is to sustain ours too. There may have been, in John's Gospel, no voice at the Baptism, no account of the Transfiguration, but Jesus has no doubt that he is 'the Son, the beloved', 'the only Son, who is close to the Father's heart'.[60]

Only love makes it possible to follow. Before the Passion, then, Peter cannot follow, even if he were to lay down his life,[61] but after the Passion Jesus allows him to affirm his love and see it as central before commissioning Peter to follow.

Obedience is then no longer a following of law. It is a response of love to a person – Christ. Discipleship is made possible by the indwelling love of Christ – the Holy Spirit. It is the work of the Holy Spirit in us which will glorify Christ through the lives of those who accept him.

I have seen the Lord

To bring this chapter to a close, we begin with Mary's words – words which are highly significant. Here is someone who has seen and believed, whose blinded sight sees beyond face value and recognises the Lord where first she saw the gardener. By that grace-empowered vision her life was changed forever.

This is John's purpose. If he has no account of the Transfiguration, it is not because he doubts it. It is rather that he sees it in the whole of Jesus' ministry. The glory of God is present not at one event and certainly not only after the Resurrection. For John it is present before the foundation of the world[62] and revealed uniquely in Jesus.

'Come and see,' he says.

Chapter 5

♦

GOD IN THE
PLACE OF ENCOUNTER

HAVING LOOKED AT the Transfiguration, we now explore the nature of encounter before turning to examine our themes in more detail in later chapters. Many of us have sympathies with St Anselm when he writes:

> Come on then, my Lord God, teach my heart where and how to seek you, where and how to find you. Lord, if you are not here, where shall I find you? If, however, you are everywhere, why do I not see you here? . . . by what signs, under what face shall I seek you? . . . What should your servant do, desperate as he is for your love yet cast away from your face? He longs to see you, and yet your face is too far away from him. He wants to come to you, and yet your dwelling place is unreachable. He yearns to discover you, and he does not know where you are. He craves to seek you, and does not know how to recognise you . . . You have made me and nurtured me, given me every good thing I have ever received, and I still do not know you. I was created for the purpose of seeing you, and I still have not done the thing I was made to do.[1]

Here St Anselm captures our dilemma. If we are made for union with God, if we are to desire to see God face to face, then how are we to find him? How do we enter this relationship with the Father and how are we to deal with his seeming absence and our inability to know him? How too are we to respond to his presence and to the knowledge we feel that we do have?

At the Transfiguration the voice from heaven says, 'This is my Son, my chosen: listen to him', and in John's Gospel Jesus seems to be saying clearly, 'I AM' the Father's Son. What lies at the heart of this relationship is a union of love. In Chapters 2–4 we have been looking at some of the background understanding of the Transfiguration in both tradition and Scripture. In this chapter we turn our thoughts towards the nature of encounter in everyday loving relationships – both with other people and with God. We recognise a pattern of initial encounter, growth of relationship, and partial union as relationships develop and as encounter happens at many levels within that relationship. We discover that in all relationships there are elements of knowing but also not knowing and that both can be helpful in establishing strong relationships. We end the chapter by recognising that the vision of God is our chief end – that vision can be complete at the end of time but is also that which most helpfully shapes our present way of living.

LOVE

In considering the initial encounter, it helps to begin with the experience of falling in love from the human perspective for, not surprisingly, the love we are to know with God has its reflection, however inadequate, in human love. Pedro Arrupe SJ writes:

> Nothing is more practical than finding God, that is, than falling in love in a quite absolute, final way.
>
> What you are in love with, what seizes your imagination, will affect everything. It will decide what will get

you out of bed in the morning, what you do with your evening, how you spend your weekends, what you read, who you know, what breaks your heart, and what amazes you with joy and gratitude.

Fall in love, stay in love and it will decide everything.[2]

But falling in love (or even falling in friendship), as many lonely people will testify, does not happen on demand. Nor is falling in love always convenient. It can challenge your deepest assumptions and deepest commitments. It presupposes that if love is to be allowed to flourish, choices affecting the whole of life will have to be made.

When eyes meet across a crowded room, as the fantasy suggests they should, there is a moment when a light dawns that a new and possibly exciting relationship may be about to begin. In this first encounter person meets person. There may be nothing known about the other person at all . . . only a sense of a deep and intuitive kinship. In this moment of gazing at another we suddenly know that a connection has been made. It may be a connection at any level, not purely a romantic or sexual one, and it may take only five minutes or a lifetime to discover what kind of relationship may develop.

In this process of discovery there will be a desire to deepen knowledge of the other. There will be sharing of life story, a sharing of experiences, an awareness of how the other reacts to life events. Even after a lifetime there may still be surprises. This gaining of knowledge is both rational and irrational, factual and intuitive, impersonal and personal. There is the gaining of certain facts – but there is also that kind of knowledge which happens when somehow the veils are removed and heart is aware of heart. Often those moments are moments of shared exultation or shared despair. They may be the joy of birth or the grief of a shared loss, shared enjoyment or shared disappointment. Again they are not predictable or within our power to organise. They are moments which happen and which later reflection may make into moments of intense insight. They may bind us together or lead us apart.

These times of reflection can be the times when love grows. Those newly in love spend hours just thinking about the other, letting what they have experienced and learnt sink deep into their consciousness and allowing it to change their life, both internally in the way that they see life and externally in the way that it is lived. It is in these times of quiet pondering that sight gives way to insight both as to the character of the other and our own character. What is true of early love can be true throughout all kinds of relationships – pondering each other may increase understanding – or at least identify where there is no understanding.

In any kind of relationship, when both parties contribute to this mutual journey and growing knowledge, so love, in its widest levels of meaning, may deepen and at times the two may feel that they are one. To develop a loving relationship, however, requires more than falling in love. Falling in love needs to give way to commitment and re-commitment. It needs to find a love which can deal with failings as well as with strengths and may even need to discover the love that is proved only in the letting go. It may indeed have to deal with loss and grief. Whilst, when we fall in love we may reveal our best self to the other (and they to us), longer-term love will reveal more of a balanced and true picture. Gonville ffrench-Beytagh writes of this 'gutsy' love:

> Love is not the sentimental easy feeling which the world thinks it is. Love can be painful, bloody and terrifying. As St Paul says, it suffers; it strips us as naked mentally as sexual intercourse strips us physically; it is not smooth and sweet and soothing – the love of romantic novelists and cooers over babies. I have often said that I wish Christians today would have a model of a bedpan round their necks and in their houses. It would convey the menial, smelly, undramatic service which love so often

demands more effectively than an ornament (the Cross) whose true meaning we have forgotten ... love is also relationship. It is taking as well as giving ... If we truly give ourselves we will find that we cannot help taking of the other's self and by some mysterious alchemy of love we always receive more than we give.[3]

If this is love – this love which serves, revealed starkly in John's Gospel by a shepherd who lays down his life, and a Master who lays aside his clothes and then his life for his friends – then it is a love which needs resourcing. For Christ and for his disciples that resourcing was the work of the Holy Spirit, a result of encounter and intimacy with God.

This pattern of encounter, growth and union is a pattern of all relationships and has been a traditional way of recognising the pattern of our coming to know God. In exploring it more fully we may reflect not only on the dynamics of making relationships but also on the way that they are resourced. If we are to understand the Transfiguration as a paradigm for encounter, we need to explore these aspects more fully.

ENCOUNTER

The initial encounter with God may be a dramatic encounter with his love and light or it may be the gradual realisation of a presence which has never before been fully recognised or admitted. That encounter, whatever it is recognised to be, is unlikely to be the first encounter that we have had. It is instead the first encounter that we have identified. Nor will it be our last encounter. We encounter God throughout our lives. Yet perhaps there have been times when we have met God's eye across a crowded room, when we have been invited to allow the veils to drop and see him as he really is. At the time we think we have encountered God in a unique way. Only later do we realise that this is the way we may encounter him again and again. Each time, though, feels like a first time, and each time we encounter a love or a mystery which takes all of us and embraces us. No longer do we imagine that we might hold God. God is holding us and yet, paradoxically, in that holding he is deeply held within us.

These glimpses of the divine may be full of visions – the kind of vision that Isaiah had in the Temple,[4] or they may be a simple awareness of the sanctity and joy of living. They do not necessarily happen in such a way as to be identifiably religious in the narrower sense of the word. There may be no angels, clouds or voices, but simply an awareness of being held in love or being held secure when life itself seems far from both. Sebastian Faulks, for instance, in his novel *On Green Dolphin Street* has a character who feels 'a sudden, lifting movement in her soul, a tide of pure compassion for her plight'; he says that 'for a few minutes she walked without feeling the ground beneath her feet; she saw herself in a true perspective, as though God loved her.'[5]

It is likely that we all have such moments but not all of us allow ourselves to be aware of them. Even those who are aware of them do not always allow them their full impact. It is not enough to have the sight, or the feeling, or the sense. We also need, as we have emphasised before, the insight necessary to allow those passing moments to be times which are enabled to change our lives.

For sight to become insight, there is both gift and endeavour. Often grace and faith are sufficient alone, but at other times we need help with interpreting what is happening ... such help may be, amongst other things, the wisdom of the Spiritual Tradition, the insights of modern study, the encouragement and interest of friends and col-leagues. No doubt those who wrote their accounts of the Gospel not only remembered what had happened but immersed themselves afresh in their Scriptures and their community of faith as they interpreted those events.

If passing encounters are to be life-changing, then we need to ponder them and to ponder the other party to the encounter in the light of all our knowledge and experience. It is here that the human parallel of being in love is most helpful. But it is not only lovers who spend hours just thinking about the beloved. It could also be said about new parents. They can spend hours holding, gazing at and enjoying the newborn child. Those hours are not wasted. Spent in love, they form the basis of the parent–child relationship and are the means by which the child's self-image and identity are affirmed and confirmed. But there are less obvious examples too – sitting by the bedside of the terminally ill, becoming aware of a neighbour or friend who needs particular care or attention. Quiet watching in love often reveals more than we, or others, imagine.

New parents, for instance, may be overjoyed that the birth was straightforward and that theirs is a beautiful baby. When they are awake at night, however, in the early days and when feeding, burping and changing nappies is not enough to settle the baby, they may begin to wonder. Were they prepared for this responsibility? Is love enough? Are they the people they thought they were? Will the baby come between them?

When they discover, later, that the cause of the baby's discomfort was simply the heat of a summer bedroom, much of their tension may be released but the questions still need an answer. In the light of their questioning and anxiety they might well become much more aware now of their responsibilities and not a little afraid. Looking at the baby might now be a more thoughtful experience, as they become more deeply aware of the true meaning of being a parent. In this gaze of love we give to the other true worth – worship – and we may also know fear. What have we got ourselves into? Am I capable of sustaining this relationship? Will it find me out to be incompetent or insincere?

True worship of God too may involve fear. We discover that depth of worship in the hours 'wasted' in gazing at God and allowing God to gaze at us. This gazing at God in love, or indeed gazing at his creation in prayerful love in order to encounter him, is described in the Spiritual Tradition as 'contemplation'. It is a radically transforming process and so may challenge us as well as delight us. Though it may increase our desire for God, it may also cause us to question our understanding of God and self. It may highlight our frailty, our unresolved history and our apparent lack of loveliness.

GROWTH IN RELATIONSHIP

What also becomes clear is that in the process of encounter, not only the parties to the encounter may be changed or affected, but the very nature of their love for each other will undergo change and transformation. When an initial encounter gives way to a longer-term relationship, love itself will be stretched, tested and strengthened as changes need to be made. It can be a costly time, for now we are seeking to love not only our first impressions of the other, nor the expectations we have projected onto them, but them as they really are. No longer can we hide behind first impressions but offer ourselves in all our glorious reality. The encounter is no longer between our 'best' selves but between our everyday selves.

When we do this there is a shattering of illusions as well as much joy in forming relationships. Some of those illusions will actually relate to the people involved in the relationship. Some will be projections of other relationships or of our own expectations. Before the Transfiguration Peter experiences this shattering of illusions. He recognises who Jesus is but his own expectation is not of a suffering Messiah, so he is not only corrected by Jesus but rebuked. Jesus cannot afford for him or us to harbour such illusions if the relationship is to be strong and enduring.[6]

In human relationships we know this suffering too when we realise that the person to whom we are committed in whatever way is not quite the person we imagined. It is then that love is tested and either grows to encompass the new

49

understanding or walks away. It is also possible that our encounters in making relationships reveal to us aspects of ourselves that strip us of illusion and challenge us by reality. Many people are content not to enter these deeper relationships – with others or with God. Those who do, know that to truly embark on the adventure is to risk a sense of falling apart as we abandon ourselves to another.

Growing in knowledge is no easy process. It is a narrow path walked sometimes with the other person but sometimes alone as we embrace all that we have learnt. Presence and absence are indeed both necessary aspects of growing in relationship, especially when there is hope not for dependency or independence but interdependency – that is, the ability to be true to oneself whilst encouraging the other to be true to themselves. Indeed, interdependency involves having both a recognised need of and enjoyment of each other.

In this growth of relationship there will be peak experiences (highs and lows) and also times when little seems to be happening. The more dramatic experiences often throw light on the whole relationship. They illumine our understanding of ourselves and of the other. Time spent reflecting on these experiences will often give us a wisdom we can gain in no other way. The spaces in between may provide the time for such reflection. They also allow us to nurture each other, to cherish the relationship and strengthen other aspects of our lives.

In parenthood, as we have seen, our self-understanding is often challenged. Roles may be changed. In a family, for instance, where husband and wife played largely conventional roles – she the home-maker and 'comforter' of the family, he the bread-winner – a life-threatening illness in their daughter changed things dramatically. When their daughter became ill it was Peter who sat by the bedside night after night. It was he who nurtured Sue, his wife, and cherished her through her anxiety, he who held the girl's hand and wiped her brow. It changed them forever. He had found in himself a need to 'cherish' and he was no longer content to be emotionally isolated. He wanted now to nurture his children and not just provide for them – to offer presence as well as presents.

As for Sue, she continued to nurture and cherish the family but she also realised that she needed some support and nurture herself – not only from Peter but from outside the family. Her days of isolation in the home gave way to study and then work, and the care of the family became more shared.

For Peter and Sue, what they had learnt about each other also affected other relationships and situations. What had come to light over those few nights of crisis threw light over the whole of their lives and their understanding of others. Peak events often have this effect. Taken further, that means that not only are the peak experiences valuable, but so are the less dramatic times, for these are the times when sight and experience give way to insight and deeper encounter. They are the times when pondering gives way to new ways of living.

The fourteenth-century mystic Meister Eckhart was keen to ask what was the use of knowing Jesus was born in Bethlehem many centuries ago if he is not born in our hearts today. What these peak experiences offer is the birth of God in us again and again, but if we have had the 'experience but missed the meaning' (as T. S. Eliot put it), then such experiences are wasted. In fact the image of birth is a good one, for if the peak experiences are the contractions of our being born in God (and he in us), then the spaces in between are times when we regroup, when we gather energy and stamina before we are encountered again. Furthermore, to return to the image of friends or lovers, these spaces in intimacy are not a denial of intimacy but the very periods that allow true intimacy to grow.

Clearly, then, the path to union with God is not a steady but an uneven one. At times we may have a profound sense of God's presence and at other times know him only by his absence. In the times of absence, in this relationship with God, as in human relationships, what keeps us strong is an awareness of our desire for another encounter and our reflection on when we have felt intimate before.

This pattern of absence and presence is most marked in, for instance, those who work for the armed services. However much husband and wife love each other, their relationship is likely to undergo dramatic change if one of them joins the army. Often one would be away from home and the other would have to fend not only for themselves but also take sole charge of the children. Such absences are likely to be both painful and illuminating. The initial sense may be of wanting to be together and the sense of 'missing the other' may dominate every thought. At other times there might be the realisation that the absence had enabled growth in each of them and both may become more competent and confident. When they are back together, the absent partner may feel marginalised and no longer needed in the same way. Absence makes presence difficult and, paradoxically, after a few weeks of presence, absence may again feel intolerable.

Similarly, our relationship with God has its absences and presences – and they too can be both gift and pain. It takes grace and faith (in human terms, mutual trust and encouragement) to stay with a relationship and allow the pains to be part of the process of bringing new life to birth rather than destruction.

Indeed, to return to childbirth and the image of encounters with God being like contractions, we are also reminded that the encounter with God may be a time not just of joy and peace but also of searing pain. So often an encounter with God is also an encounter with our deepest self. It is both the time when we become aware of our deepest need and frailty, but also aware most fully of the hope of healing contained in the assurance of God's faithfulness and grace. Our suffering then is not suffering for its own sake but the suffering which leads to birth, the suffering by which we are stripped of all that is false and by which we reclaim all that is most true in us. This process depends on God's faithfulness and our response, God's gift and our receptivity.

The only way in which relationships can dare to go beyond these times of stripping, illusion-blowing and deepening reality is to know that each is committed to the other with a tender yet courageous love. Unless such love is assured, it is almost impossible, and inadvisable, to take the risks of deeper self-disclosure that such a journey entails.

Relationship also depends on a holding together of past, present and future. The past and our response to it has made our relationship what it is. It has impact on the present. Our hopes too shape the present. Commitment in love is, in a sense, a holding on to what is to be and using that vision of the future as a means of shaping the here and now. By committing oneself to another, one is simply saying that one wants the future 'union' to be worked out in the future and 'seeds' of it to be found in the present.

Growing in relationship with God is not so different from growing in relationship with other people. We need this shared commitment to the future and a vision of what is possible. The Transfiguration is one such vision. It revealed Jesus in a new way to Peter, James and John. The familiar friend became awesome to look at – God the Creator revealing himself in a man in such a way as to attract their devotion for a lifetime – a vision which revealed not only the glory of God but the depth of his committed love, his steadfast love.

In human relationships what follows on from an act of commitment and shared vision depends on love and that growth in trust which comes from shared knowledge and experience. What makes God different from any human love relationship is the absolute certainty of his love for us. To respond to this attraction of the beauty and love of God is, however, to risk becoming aware of our own weight holding us back. Peter continues to be our prime example, for Peter is swept up to God by the experience of the Transfiguration as he looks at Jesus. Yet Peter is then held back by his weight as he recognises his fear and so denies Jesus. He is able to walk on water when he looks at Jesus, but sinks when he sees the storm and wind.

Discipleship, then, is not about an easy walking of the path that Jesus has trodden. It is rather to walk our own path in identification with Jesus. It is to learn to live through the sense of absence as well as presence, to keep desire strong when experience is missing. There is a cost as well as a joy in discipleship, and it is often when the cost becomes apparent that discipleship either falls away or becomes superficial. Instead, if we want to encounter God more deeply, we need to learn to use the struggle and to live through it in much the same way that we discover in human relationships. For it is then that we find ourselves growing closer to those whom we love.

UNION

The Westminster Catechism, in response to the question, 'What is the chief and highest end of man (*sic*)?' gave the answer, 'Man's chief and highest end is to glorify God and fully enjoy him for ever'; and St Ignatius writes, 'Man is created to praise, reverence, and serve God our Lord, and by this means to save his soul. The other things on the face of the earth are created for man to help him in attaining the end for which he was created.'[7]

We are made to live in relationship with God and to bring glory to him not by fearing him but by enjoying him and enjoying all that he has made. The initiative for this adventure of love is not ours but God's. Nevertheless, it requires of us a response, a consent to what God wants to do in us and through us. The consent is reflected in Jesus' attitude to the Father – one of pure receptivity, of total devotion, of freedom to be himself and of love for others. He reveals to us that union with God does not destroy oneself but completes oneself. We are not lost in God but loved in God, not submerged in God but glorified in God.

If we desire such union, there is both an active and a passive facet to our response to God. Sometimes we have to be proactive and at other times allow God to set not only the agenda but the pace of our coming together. Of all the spiritual writers, John of the Cross sets out these elements of encounter most clearly. He recognises that in the early stages (to which we may return at times) we have to consciously decide to make God the centre of our life and attention. We will need to develop disciplines of prayer and life which reflect our desire to come closer to God. In much the same way, if we want a human relationship to grow, we give time and attention to the other. In all relationships this is not just in order to come to a point of commitment but needs to be ongoing if the commitment is to bear fruit in growing intimacy and love.

Within that structure of committed love, however, there is a deeper consent which truly allows the other to shape us so that by their love they strip us of illusion and reveal to us more truly who we are. This is the more passive aspect of consent and by far the more costly, for it implies a lack of control and a trust in the other which is easier to affirm in words than it is in action.

This is when falling in love for fun becomes 'falling in love in a quite absolute, final way'.[8] Sometimes it is by choice and sometimes life circumstances throw us into this level of loving, when, for instance, one partner becomes ill so as to need long-term practical care.[9] In terms of our relationship with God, it is the way of abandonment summed up beautifully in Charles de Foucauld's prayer:

> My Father, I abandon myself to you.
> Do with me what you will.
> Whatever you may do I thank you.
> I am prepared for anything, I accept anything.

Provided your will is fulfilled in me and in all
creatures I ask for nothing more, my God.
I place my soul in your hands.
I give it to you, my God,
with all the love of my heart
because I love you.
And for me it is a necessity of love,
this gift of myself,
this placing of myself in your hands
without reserve
in boundless confidence
because you are my Father.[10]

But, more importantly, it was also summed up in his life. It is when people allow God to enter into this dynamic centre of their being and to touch them with love that abandonment comes – not a turgid following of duty, not a masochistic self-giving but rather an opening up to an encounter which both strips and heals us.

That encounter is not in the refined air of a supposed spiritual elite but in the daily encounters of life. It is in the texture of the often-ignored threads of our humdrum life. We are to find God not by going in search of him elsewhere but by waiting patiently on him and finding him within. As George Aschenbrenner says, 'we can find and taste and smell and touch a God mysteriously and wonderfully labouring and loving to the end.'[11]

And perhaps this is the real challenge for people who desire God, for we share with many the inability 'to encounter reality face to face',[12] but it is essential that we do, for 'Faith is not something we acquire once and for all. Faith is an insight that must be acquired at every single moment.'[13]

Here we strike the heart of the matter: that discipleship is not so much about what we believe or say but about how we encounter God in the daily events of life. The peak experiences, like the Transfiguration, are to illumine how we live in the darkness as well as in the light. They are a glimpse of how God intends us to see him, and we must live towards that vision.

Faith, then, is nurtured by living in the present moment, aware of its potential, learning from its lesson and receiving its grace. To return to John's Gospel, this was precisely the point of the signs. They are to promote faith to those who have eyes to see and insight to discover.

But again we must emphasise that there is, for us, an element of 'now and not yet'. We both know and yet do not know fully. We still have partial vision until we see God face to face. Our moments of seeing his glory give way sometimes to finding only darkness. Our knowledge of God becomes not just what we can positively affirm but also recognising our limitations – our 'unknowing'. As John of Damascus says, 'God is infinite and incomprehensible and all that is comprehensible about him is his infinity and his incomprehensibility.'[14] To put it more simply, we can often only describe God by saying, 'He is like this . . .' whilst recognising that whatever we have said is completely false because however much God is 'like this', he is also wholly other. So we may say God is like a loving father, but we also have to recognise that he is unlike any earthly father we have known.

This is not to confuse us but to help us recognise ourselves as creatures of a loving Creator who both reveals and conceals his true self as best suits our journey towards him. Our union and our knowledge are necessarily incomplete and neither is increased in a straightforward way. Rather, we ebb and flow in knowledge, experience and love. Nevertheless, if we desire union and knowledge, then our desire and God's desire transfigure the whole of life as we become more aware.

AWARENESS

A lady whose family life had been traumatic, and which had resulted in the accidental death of her husband as a result of a blow from their son in the heat of an argument, wrote afterwards:

> My heartbreak rises up and almost submerges me at times ... I am going to try harder to just keep looking at the Lord, look directly at him ... I believe it is our awareness of Christ that can help others, sick ones too, since we are all in touch through the subconscious.[15]

Here is someone who has learnt that the only way to deal with life is to be in love with God and to gaze at him, not to avoid the pain of life but in order not to allow bitterness and despair to conquer faith and love. Gazing at God would not automatically put things right for her. Nothing could do that. But gazing at God would shape the way that she handled the future and what she would learn in the process. In her gazing at God she would be challenged about her response to her son and to others. Quite simply, she was making herself aware of God in a situation where one might expect her to give up faith. She was committed to growing through the pain because she was committed to God.

If we want to grow in faith, we need to train our vision to gaze at God – to gaze at God in the time we give to prayer, and to gaze at God as we meet him in other people. Our prayer and life then is a whole – one in which we gaze at God – but our prayer time, that time which we set apart for God, is often the time when our vision is renewed so that we might have the sight to see him in other people too.

If prayer can help us to become more aware, then prayerful reflection on life is often the way to gain insight. Simply reflecting on the events of the day can unfold levels of meaning that are not apparent as we live the day. That insight gained of course refines our vision again. In such reflection we learn from the experiences of life and receive their gifts of grace. Our daily encounters become symbolic and part of our encounter with the living God.

What the woman's life also makes clear is that those

encounters are not less than real. They contain their share not only of the joy of living but also of the pain of living. They may contain blessing but also deep wounding. They may speak of union with God but also make clear our distinction from God as creatures of the Creator. In our awareness and in our reflection these aspects all have their place. Growth in faith therefore also demands that we understand the necessity of healing as a part of the journey of faith.

Indeed, Russ Parker writes of healing as a journey, in company with others, leading us to God.[16] If we are to find union with God, then we most often need the company of others – our awareness and reflection may need their prayer and ministry as well as their human support and companionship. No wonder, then, that on the Mount of Transfiguration and in the Garden of Gethsemane Jesus has Peter, James and John with him. In the naked encounter with glory or with grief we are drawn to realise the necessity of human as well as divine support and grace.

In this chapter we have seen that to encounter God is to learn how to love and be loved. We have recognised the cost as well as the joy of that. We have recognised the need of others as well as travelling the lone journey. In the following chapters we explore those themes already identified which mark this encounter.

We began with St Anselm. We end with some words of St Irenaeus:

> By our own powers we cannot see God, yet God will be seen by us because he wills it. He will be seen by those he chooses at the time he chooses, and in the way he chooses, for God can do all things ... As those who see light are in the light sharing its brilliance, so those who see God are in God sharing his glory, and that glory gives them life. To see God is to share life.[17]

Chapter 6

♦

THE PLACE OF ENCOUNTER: KNOWING CHRIST

> No longer shall they teach one another, or say to each other 'Know the Lord', for they shall all know me, from the least of them to the greatest.
>
> *Jeremiah 31:34*

I AM STANDING ON THE BEACH and the sea is coming towards me. I know the sea very well . . . and have watched it for ages. But now the waves are lapping around my feet and my knowledge is different. I am experiencing the sea in a different way. I am no longer an observer but a participant and, should the wave overwhelm me, I will be swept away.

Gaining knowledge is very much like standing on the shore. We can *gain knowledge* by observing and learning *about* that which we wish to know. We can *participate in* what we want to know, or encounter the person we wish to know, or we can *be abandoned* to what we know. Whatever our response, we will gain in knowledge.

The sea is a good image too because it portrays the fear we have, not of knowing, but of being known. If we dare to encounter God, are we prepared to be known fully by him? And, more, are we prepared in that knowledge to be changed by him, transfigured in him?

In this chapter we explore what it means to know God and

60

be known by him, looking first at the scriptural understanding of knowing, then at our desire to know God and our ability to both know and not know until the ultimate face-to-face encounter with God. We look at our resistance to knowing and being known, our reluctance to being changed, and our need of God's grace.

THAT THEY MAY KNOW YOU

When Jesus prays to the Father that he may be glorified and so glorify the Father, he prays for those who believe, that they may share the glory of eternal life – a life which means that they may *know* the Father. Indeed, from the beginning of time humankind was to know God and be known by him.[1] Such knowledge was to be gained by experience, by observation and reflection, or by learning.[2] In Deuteronomy people are encouraged to consider how God had carried them as a father carries a child to bring them to safety.[3] Such reflection of first-hand experience is to help them know more about the nature and purposes of their faithful and loving God.[4]

At other times we learn not directly by experiencing God's tenderness but by a more impersonal reflection. So, for example, Noah, seeing the dove come back with an olive leaf, knew that the floods had subsided.[5] We learn too by instruction and by relating that instruction to our own experience of living by it. No wonder then that in later Judaism the rabbis related 'knowing God' to knowing the Law.

To know God is to learn in all these ways. It is to learn and respond not only with the mind but with the heart, but equally not only with the heart but with the mind – and with our soul and strength. It is to know and love with the whole of our being.

It is true too that though we can desire to know God, we cannot know him unaided. We know God because he chooses to reveal himself (through what we have earlier called faith and grace). We may gain intuitive knowledge of God by love and intellectual knowledge by prayerful study and reflection. It is, however, likely that we will soon discover that the more we articulate our knowledge of God, the more we realise how difficult it is to convey God in words, for though he is indeed very close to us and within us, he is also far greater than us. To presume we know God completely is to have lost God and created an idol. It is to have exchanged the transfiguring search for God for a dull complacency.

The transfiguring search, the transforming encounter, are the ebb and flow of the spiritual journey – the living of our life in the conscious knowledge of the presence of God. Such knowledge may be at times a felt presence. At other times it will be a faithful living out of what we have learnt even when we feel, hear, or see nothing of God.

We tread warily then towards deepening our knowledge of God, letting God reveal himself as he will whilst we make time and opportunity to learn what he will teach us. The unknown author of *The Cloud of Unknowing* comes to our aid:

> learn to love God with quiet, eager joy, at rest in body as in soul. Remember your manners and wait humbly upon our Lord's will. Do not snatch upon it, like some famished dog, however much you hunger for it.[6]

There is a proper and natural reticence in wanting to know God, a respect which allows God to reveal himself and does not presume to rush. It is a lifetime's work and a work which will help us not only know God but come to know ourselves in new and often challenging ways. In our coming to know God we will be transfigured into glory,[7] but to know God in this way will take us, like Paul, through the full human experience of life – the full Paschal mystery.[8] There will be suffering and joy, times of darkness as well as light, and these are all to be expected. It is in all of this that we are transfigured. The change in us will often be hidden, often inconsistent and unbearably slow. It takes much courage and grace to stay with the process. It demands a continuing and repeated consent to the will of God.[9] No wonder then that many shy away from it or fall away, not recognising the challenge to consent again and again. Teilhard de Chardin helps us when he says:

Above all, trust in the slow work of God.
We are, quite naturally,
impatient in everything to reach the end
without delay.
We should like to skip
the intermediate stages.
We are impatient of being
on the way to something unknown,
something new.
And yet it is the law of all progress
that it is made by passing through
some stages of instability –
And that it may take a very long time.

And so I think it is with you.
Your ideas mature gradually –
let them grow,
let them shape themselves,
without undue haste.
Don't try to force them on,
as though you could be today
what time (that is to say, grace and
circumstances acting
on your own good will)
will make you tomorrow.

Only God could say what this new spirit
gradually forming within you will be.
Give our Lord the benefit of believing that his hand is
    leading you,

and accept the anxiety of
feeling yourself in suspense and incomplete.[10]

This very sense of being incomplete is in fact our greatest
help, for it highlights our restlessness and the frustration of
the desire which itself is the key to our growth. It is this
awareness of a longing to grow that enables us to be open to
seeing more clearly and which prepares us for those encounters which may become the bedrock of our faith,[11] through
which we have come to see and know Christ and our world
in new and life-changing ways.

These encounters may be nothing more than the everyday
circumstances of our lives – but seen through the eyes of
faith, they are the encounters which reveal God's presence in
his world to those who are aware . . . reminders that although
we may not see God face to face in this life, we may nevertheless see glimpses of his glory.[12]

TO KNOW AND YET NOT KNOW

St John's Gospel, in particular, draws us to a sense of 'now
and not yet'. In Jesus we see God's glory and yet we shall
not see it fully until after the events of Jesus' passion, death
and resurrection. Here we have a double hope – that we shall
see God's glory in Christ when we see him at the end of time
– what is called the beatific vision – but that we may also see
signs of glory in this life. This presents us with a challenge.
As Thomas Merton says:

I believe that he has called me freely, out of pure mercy,
to his Love and salvation and that at the end (to which
all is directed by him) I shall see Him after I have put off
my body in death and have risen together with Him . . . I
am even now in the Kingdom and I can even now 'see'
something of the glory of the Kingdom and praise him
who is King. I would be foolish then if I lived blindly,

putting all 'seeing' off until some imagined fulfillment (for my present seeing is the beginning of a real and unimaginable fulfillment!).[13]

The challenge is then about the choices we make and about our level of awareness of the presence and activity of God now. It is about the meaning we give to religious experience, and the way in which we deal with faith and life when, though we believe, we apparently have no such experience.

> In a Dorset village there lives a devout old lady whom I shall call Lucy. She set ten eggs under a broody hen. She was not sure whether they were fertile, the old cock-bird had been roaming about the yard so they might be, but it was all a little haphazard and un-scientific. Two days later the broody escapes from the coop, wanders off for a scratch and a spot of exercise, gets herself entangled in a bramble and cannot get back. Lucy finds her, disentangles her, and pops her back on the eggs, but with misgivings, things are going wrong. Three days later there is a violent storm, hail and water pour into the coop, the hen is distracted, distressed and soaked, and in the morning Lucy finds that three of the eggs are chipped. So it goes on for twenty days, mishap after mishap, until the old lady wonders whether it is worthwhile going on with the project but having got so far she might as well leave things for another day.
>
> On the twenty-first morning, Lucy looked with calm and controlled surprise at ten healthy little chicks gambolling around in the sunshine, and her reaction is spontaneous: It is the Lord! Silly sentimental superstitious old dear . . .[14]

But having told Lucy's story, Martin Thornton goes on to compare her reaction with the beloved disciple and the catch of 153 fish. He helpfully suggests that for John and the early Church such experiences of the Lord were *evidential*. They were indeed the evidence of the risen Lord. For us such experiences are not easily made evidential – too easily when we articulate them they lose their distinctive and life-giving qualities that so moved us. Nor can we hold on to them, as Peter learnt at the Transfiguration and we may learn in our own. Ann Lewin's poem 'Transfiguration' is helpful at this point:

> A moment of blinding perception –
> It would be good to stay there,
> But clutch it and it's gone.
> They come unheralded,
> These moments of dazzling clarity,
> And leave us as suddenly.
>
> As well to try to catch the kingfisher
> Darting through stillness.
>
> Be thankful for its jewelled beauty,
> And keep awake, alert.[15]

We cannot clutch at such experiences but we can reflect on them. Then, as Thornton says, they are for us *strengthening*, *sustaining* and *renewing*.[16]

They are also spasmodic and episodic. We cannot say when, where or how we will become aware of God. We may gently expect to see him but find him in the unexpected rather than the expected places.

We may expect to find God through worship, prayer and Scripture and then find him instead in an unexpected meeting or a casual conversation. We may gain a degree in Theology and then find God in giving birth. God is not to be pinned down. Nevertheless, if we choose to seek God in Christ then, as in any search, we will make ourselves aware of what is already known of our quarry. We build up an impression of the one we seek. Prayer, worship, study and the reading of Scripture may help us build up this impression, but they cannot and will not be a substitute for an encounter with the risen Lord.[17]

If we are seeking God, it can only be because he is first seeking us (and first loved us, 1 John 4:10), and it would be foolish to ignore the means of coming to know him that he has already given. A simple, open-eyed and free reading of the Gospels may be all that it takes to see Jesus for who he is and then recognise a family likeness in people we encounter. Indeed, every time we encounter real love we will be encountering him.

This choice to seek God in Christ will change our way of seeing life. It will make us more aware of the presence of God, not just in our encounters with other people but in our encounters with the whole of life. This everyday awareness is perhaps our greatest gift and ally. It prepares us for those dramatic encounters, should they come our way, when the blindness seems to be lifted from our eyes. Peter knew those moments especially when he saw who Jesus was – first when Jesus asked and then when Jesus gave him the vision of the Transfiguration.

Such experiences of the closeness of God may be few in number in our lives and they are difficult to capture in order to explain them to other poeple. For Peter the Transfiguration was clearly, as we have said, an event of enormous impact and a profound marker of his apostolic witness. They were understood by the writer of 2 Peter as evidential and the use of such writings in the early Church and then their inclusion in the canon of Scripture gave further weight to such experiences as evidence.

Our experience, however, is seldom evidential in this way. It is much more likely that our experience is in order to strengthen, sustain and renew our faith. Our experience of God is to be enjoyed for what it is and it needs to be set free to do what it alone can do – transform and transfigure us.

Often in our haste to witness to God's activity in our lives we set in stone an event which was given to us not so much as to pass on for itself but to change us. To be changed by such experiences involves reflection on the experience and making choices in the light of that experience. It is when the experience has touched the depth of our being that it will transform us.[18] There is then a necessary delay between our experience of God and our articulation of it, even to ourselves. It is in the delay that we discover the meaning.

Finally, on the question of not having experience of God, it will be clear from the above that we believe that we all have experience of God, whether it be in becoming aware of day-to-day goodness and love, or in being aware of specific encounters where God seems especially close. Those experiences may be *spiritual* ones – where we become aware of something/someone greater than ourselves which questions the meaning of our existence – or, because of our own beliefs we may recognise them to be *religious* experiences – that is, ones that relate to a specific faith tradition.

RESISTANCE AND RELUCTANCE

Peter, of all the disciples, shows us how we can both want to know and be reluctant to know. He is first to answer Jesus' question, 'Who do you say that I am?'[19] but he is also the one who rebukes Jesus for imparting the further knowledge that the Messiah must suffer. He may have the insight to know who Jesus really is, but he has yet to have the further sight and insight to know about the passive ministry of Christ – his suffering.

This points to a human reality – that however deeply we feel we know another person, there can yet be surprises. It is as though we are all diamonds with many facets. Even though we may see deeply through one of more facets with what feels like intense clarity, we are in fact only seeing part of the whole. Fuller knowledge is gained not just by reflection on one insight but by being prepared to gain more, to have our eyes opened again and again and our image of the other changed and changed again.

In coming to know another person – and in coming to know God – there are, perhaps, four avenues of approach. There is the sharing of life in all of its complexity, being alongside each other in facing what life brings and in trying to understand its meaning for us. Secondly, there is 'playing together' – a sharing of leisure time and unstructured time together – relaxation and leisure which give us other insights into the other person. Thirdly, there is the spontaneous – the sudden new insight which is pure gift and may be pure challenge. Finally, there is the ability to grow through mis-understanding and failure (apparent and real). Clearly, this is a gross simplification but nevertheless may help us as we seek to understand what it means to know God and be changed by that knowledge.

A relationship with God needs all of these aspects if it is to be part of a transfiguring search. It is as if the relationship with God needs a certain etiquette once the introductions have been made, not to restrict either God or the person but actually to create the freedom in which the optimum relationship may develop and real change be effected.

In terms of our four avenues of approach, we may see how the life of faith can help us approach God:

1. In facing life together with God, the faith community itself may help us find a structure for our journey. Worship, liturgy and meeting with fellow believers who share our faith tradition may give us a framework of beliefs which help us to understand and interpret our experience. Personal prayer too helps us relate our relationship with God to our daily life. None of these, however, can be said to be the means by which relationship happens. They are not. All relationships, however hard we work at them, are, in the end, gift, and this is no different. However, these activities, shared with others, create an attitude in us that says

clearly that we want our desire for God to have space and we want our desire for God to have credence in our life.

2. Beyond this 'scaffolding', however, there is a relationship with God which will be a personal relationship and will have its own dynamic and its own vitality. It will therefore claim attention during the events of each day. It will show itself in our being aware at times throughout the day of the overriding claims of God. Short 'arrow prayers' may pierce the mists of our day and God may at times break upon us as sunlight which scatters those same mists. To be aware of God breaking upon us, we may cultivate an attitude of waiting:

> Prayer is like watching for the
> Kingfisher. All you can do is
> Be where he is likely to appear, and
> Wait.
> Often, not much happens;
> There is space, silence and
> Expectancy.
> No visible sign, only the
> Knowledge that he's been there,
> And may come again.
> Seeing or not seeing cease to matter,
> You have been prepared.
> But sometimes, when you've almost
> Stopped expecting it,
> A flash of brightness
> Gives encouragement.[20]

3. There is then the spontaneous, which, however much we have waited, is pure gift – being 'surprised by joy' to quote a C. S. Lewis phrase. In fact these later two are more about play than work. They can be lighthearted and often happen as a result of relaxation and creativity. For this reason it is

good to remember that life is prayer and that having fun is also part of living with God.

4. But there also needs to be a way of working though misunderstanding and failure, not to be held back by guilt. We need to be prepared to enter the Father's embrace and be covered in glory even when we know ourselves to have been far away.[21]

GRACE

Often peoples' resistance to God is shown in their resistance and reluctance to make time for prayer, in their refusal to believe that God enjoys them so much that he wants them to enjoy him and his creation, or in their inability to believe not only in a loving God but in a truly forgiving God.

Even those who do commit themselves to prayer and who long for God deeply discover levels of resistance and reluctance they might earlier have thought impossible for them. That resistance is often related to our image of God and our understanding of him. If God is drawing us to himself then there can still be a dread of coming closer. It may be that we believe in a God of love in our head and yet our heart still relates to a different image – an image learnt earlier in life, or in other circumstances – which may not be loving. Who would want to be drawn to a God who is not loving?

Even a loving God can however create resistance in us if we are ashamed of who we are or what we have done. There can be enormous conflict in us as we seek to draw closer to a God who we know loves us but who seems to have made us 'not quite right'. For those who feel 'unacceptable' to themselves, their family and friends or society this can seem an insuperable difficulty. We may feel that coming closer to God will tear us apart rather than free us . . . for God calls us to himself and draws us to searing honesty about ourselves – an impossible challenge in the light of our personal circumstances.

What then is this struggle about? It is often the struggle of the deepest self to find acceptance, love and a sense of value. That longing which is primarily and most truly a longing for God may find fulfillment in all sorts of ways which satisfy us for a while but may ultimately betray us. We call some of them addictions – alcohol, drugs, gambling – but the reality is that we all have ways of dealing with our longing for love and belonging.

Maybe our childhood filled up our reservoir and our longing is less insistent and more free as a result. But it may be that childhood wounds and adolescent fears have left us with a longing that demands to be filled and which we have learnt either to repress or to satisfy with ways which are more or less acceptable to us and to society. Without any judgemental connotations, we may call them all addictions. They are ways of living that we have discovered originally to help us maintain a sense of equilibrium. Only when they have become too demanding of us and have become self-destructive addictions do they create dis-equilibrium for us and for others.

Being drawn closer to God may challenge some of these ways of living . . . not necessarily because they are wrong in themselves but because they hold us back from living more fully and more freely. They are like ropes that hold us down whilst God is trying to lift us up. As St John of the Cross says, it does not matter whether they are ropes or thin cords. If they hold us back from God, they need to be broken if we are to be changed, transfigured.

Such change is painful and may require an amount of grieving if we are to let go of ways of living and coping that have become habitual over long periods. Again the sudden and dramatic has given way to process and slow change.

We need too to be aware of what it means to release the ropes. It is not necessarily a matter of abandoning what is important to us – whether that be people, situations or possessions, nor even our desire for them – but rather discovering a freedom in handling them. It is not a letting go of what is important to us, but a letting go of possessive attachment. Even this is a costly challenge. It is no wonder then that there is reluctance and resistance.

This then is one source – the attachments we have where our longing for God has been fixed on other attractions. There is another source of resistance which is simply the fear of being hurt. Being prepared to change is to be prepared for the unknown. It carries the risk of hurt. We are made vulnerable not only to God's love but to the full rigours of life and to the pain of all that we have already said about letting go of attachments. The fear of being hurt may be more hidden and less accessible to change.

Against our resistance and reluctance, however, is *grace*. Grace is God's free gift by which we may be changed. Gerald C. May comments:

> Grace is the most powerful force in the universe. It can transcend repression, addiction and every other internal or external power that seeks to oppress the freedom of the human heart. Grace is where our hope lies.[22]

Grace, however powerful and free, needs our co-operation. It is not a gift to release us from responsible living but rather the means by which we live most responsibly and freely in relationship with God. Grace enables us to stay with the reality of our situation but make choices about living in the light of our awareness of the help, will and goodness of God. Grace does not wait for God to do what we can choose and set out to do. Grace recognises that we can do it only with God's help. Grace means too that we will be content to move forward at God's pace and in God's time.

Grace is what enables us to do what we cannot do for ourselves. A good image is that of mountaineers who help each other climb heights impossible for the single climber. In very practical terms that is what we may call *human* grace. It is often by human grace that we are empowered to let go of our restrictive past and find a greater freedom. It is especially important through times of transition and change or when we are unable to help ourselves for whatever reason.

Grace is the means of our transformation. To be transfigured by God is to allow grace free play within our deepest being. In the Spiritual Tradition, then, it has always been important to be as free as possible from attachments to false 'gods'. As Gerald C. May says, 'Our addictions fill up the spaces within us, spaces where grace might flow.'[23]

The task then is threefold – to make space for God in our lives, to let God go beyond what we can do for ourselves and make more space for himself (the stripping of illusions and false attachments), and to live as if we are already filled with grace even before it feels like a reality. This is to live in the belief that we are ultimately and wholly loved by God even if, for the present, we do not feel such love. This divine love needs to be affirmed too by our companions on the journey as we encourage each other to persevere. Only by God's grace do we know God most fully and only by his grace will we see him face to face.

In this chapter we have explored what it means to know God – from outer knowledge and then finally by inner grace. That knowledge may lead us to worship and fear.

Chapter 7

♦

THE PLACE OF ENCOUNTER:
WORSHIP AND FEAR

A learned man lost all his sources of income and was
looking for a way to earn a living. The members of his
community, who admired him for his learning and piety,
suggested to him to serve as their cantor on the Days of
Awe. But he considered himself unworthy of serving as
the messenger of the community, as the one who should
bring the prayers of his fellow men to the Almighty. He
went to his friend, the Rabbi of Husiatim and told him
of his sad plight, of the invitation to serve as Cantor on
the Days of Awe, and of his being afraid to accept it and
pray for his congregation.

'Be afraid and pray', was the answer of the Rabbi.

Abraham Heschel[1]

THE ENCOUNTER WITH GOD inculcates awe and fear as well
as worship. In this chapter we see how the Transfiguration
is a paradigm of such encounters. We look again at the symbolic elements of the story – the mountain, light, cloud and
voice – and then at the whole concept of worship and its
accompanying fear.

The accounts of the Transfiguration hold together insights
of Jesus which show his transcendence as well as his immanence. What happens on the mountain is not an everyday

experience. The disciples are led to see the glory of God in a human face – the majesty of God in a close friend. Their being there was crucial for, in their perception and acceptance of the moment – 'It is good that we are here' – they added their voice to the heavenly one. For Jesus, all the voices he heard would have confirmed his own insight into what was to come – the glory would necessarily give way to suffering but also to a greater glory. Words and voices were vitally important but beyond words were those symbols which carry a deep relevance and meaning.

SYMBOLS

Symbols are often taken for granted. They create the setting of our existence and may have different meanings for different people and cultures. Even those who try to avoid symbols as being idolatrous actually discover that certain objects or ways of doing things become important to them. This is particularly true in the area of worship. Whether it be the candles and incense of one tradition or the well-thumbed Bible of another, symbols evoke, carry and create meaning.

In the accounts of the Transfiguration, symbols are especially important and it may be helpful to review their meanings again.[2]

The mountain

For Jesus and the disciples the high mountain would have been significant. Mountains in their faith tradition played a crucial part. The binding of Isaac took place on Moriah (later identified with Zion), the Torah was given to Moses on Sinai, and Elijah struggled with the prophets of Baal on Carmel. The presence of Elijah and Moses at the Transfiguration on a mountain is therefore strongly indicative of the importance of what is happening. The voice from heaven speaking of

Jesus as the Son has, perhaps, echoes of the binding of Isaac, where he is described erroneously as Abraham's *only* son.[3]

Alongside these specific incidents from the tradition, mountains were often seen as places where God dwelt and from where help would come.[4] They were places of encounter and worship not only with the LORD God but also with other gods. In time, then, there was a move to centralise worship[5] not on any mountain but in Jerusalem and on Mount Zion.

The fact that the Transfiguration takes place on a mountain is therefore highly significant. It is a place of revelation, of encounter and of drama.

The light

From the dawn of creation to the vision of the everlasting city, light is the prerogative of God. It is his first creation and his own gift – a sign of his presence. For later Christians light became symbolic of Jesus too, who refers to himself as the light of the world. As Peter, James and John looked at this friend of theirs, the experience of radiant light revealed Jesus as divine. Time – past, present and future – was held in the radiance of his glory. The past was fulfilled, the present affirmed and the future assured.

The cloud

If God is known in light, he can also be known in darkness. Indeed, Moses found him there – 'then the people stood at a distance, while Moses drew near to the thick darkness, where God was.'[6] Cloud on mountains is often experienced as darkness rather than light and so even at the human level it is no wonder that Luke speaks of the disciples being afraid as they entered the cloud. The cloud, though, has other levels of significance. It is a symbol of revelation and glory. 'The cloud is not itself the glory but . . . [it] is a covering which conceals the glory which shines through it from within.'[7] Again, the cloud speaks of transcendence and immanence. The cloud suggests that God is immanent and yet the glory which the cloud points to and embraces is wholly other – transcendent. Sight may lead to fear of darkness but insight will inculcate a deeper fear – the awe and fear at God's presence.

The voice

Whilst for Mark and Luke the disciples become afraid at the cloud, for Matthew it is the voice as well which induces fear and leads them to fall on their faces. Matthew draws on Old Testament passages where fear is expressed and where people fall to the ground.[8] Clearly the voice is a marker of divine presence and the disciples' reaction is of corresponding intensity. Again there is revelation but also indications of the future glory.

All these symbols, then, remind us that in the Transfiguration the past is fulfilled in a present epiphany which indicates and foreshadows a future and final revelation of glory. These symbols go beyond words. They take us to the heart of the divine. The setting of worship is not about the symbols themselves. The setting of worship is the presence of the divine.

Worship is about the encounter with a God who is both transcendent and immanent. It is a reaching beyond the fear that accompanies the sacred to the 'unknown' but intimate and loving God. It is entering the cloud in the hope of glory. It has an inner and outer aspect.

Worship is also intimately connected with all that it means to be human. The greatest symbol of the Transfiguration (though 'symbol' is too feeble a word) is Jesus himself, and it is perhaps the figure of Jesus as revealed at the Transfiguration that most informs our attitude to worship.

The Jewish scholar Abraham Heschel writes that it is

perhaps significant that the Hebrew word that came to

denote the symbol 'semel' occurs in the Bible five times but always in a derogatory sense, denoting an idolatrous object . . . and yet there is something in the world that the Bible does regard as a symbol of God . . . man, every man . . . man must therefore be greeted with the honour due to a likeness representing the King of Kings.[9]

Heschel also invites us to treat ourselves as symbols of God. In the Transfiguration Jesus shows us that we are such a 'symbol'. By revealing God's glory though his humanity, he reveals what is also our destiny and hope. He thus enables us to discover the divine *within* ourselves as we contemplate the divine *beyond* ourselves. In that resonance of divine with divine, worship is inevitable. The Transfiguration also makes clear that in Christ divinity is not exclusive of full humanity. For ourselves, to be fully aware of the divine within would be to be fully human. In his humanity Jesus also reveals in the Transfiguration what it is to say 'Yes' to God, and in his 'Yes' we may make our own. This is the other side of worship – the willingness not only to listen but to obey, not only to hear but to do.

WORSHIP

Worship is primarily a response to the living God. In that sense it cannot be entirely ordered and directed by us. It has elements of the spontaneous, of duty tempered by love, and of an inward attitude. Above all worship is about living as well as about liturgy.

If worship is a response to the living God, then it is at times worship for God's sake alone. At its highest, worship is a response beyond words to the infinite mystery, majesty and intimate and embracing love of God, and when this worship is encountered, then transfiguration follows. In the story of Job we see such a moment. Having questioned himself and God, Job comes to a point where his arguments give way to presence and he says, 'I had heard of you by the hearing of an ear, but now my eye sees you; therefore I despise myself, and repent in dust and ashes.'[10] Similarly Isaiah finds himself caught up in worship and he too sees only his need of cleansing.[11] Most significantly, Ezekiel, whose vision of God is so often a figure 'like a human being' surrounded by fire and brightness, recognises that transformation can only come about by God's desire. It is this holy God who will 'sprinkle clean water upon you . . . A new heart I will give you, and a new spirit I will put within you.'[12]

This encounter with the Transcendent God is powerful, life-changing and fearful, for it appears that this Holy God, jealous for his own holiness, cannot and will not be thwarted by the rebellious blindness of his people. Clearly, here is a cause for fear as well as hope. The presence of the living God is the presence of utter holiness and transcendence. In relation to the Transfiguration this has its own significance for Peter especially. It is Peter who, when Jesus encourages the fishermen to throw the nets once more into the deep,[13] recognises who Jesus is and falls at his feet saying, 'Go away from me, LORD for I am a sinful man', and who, with the others, is encouraged by Jesus not to fear. How much more focused, awesome and fearful must the sight of the transfigured Jesus have been for him. When God is revealed spontaneously through everyday life, it is his holiness which evokes fear and change.

But for Peter and for us, these times of being surprised by God's revelations cannot be separated from a life of prayer and worship which may at times seem mundane and dry. Indeed, the Transfiguration is clearly an example of the spontaneous, but in another sense it is part of the pattern of prayer and worship which Jesus has already established with the disciples. Its power is not so much in what happened as in what the disciples (and the evangelists and their readers) make of what happened – their inward attitude which, as we have already seen, expressed itself in fear, awe and worship.

Part of that reaction was spontaneous but it was a spontaneity shaped and coloured by a lifetime of worship and a time of being with Jesus in the ordinary. If they had eyes to see, it was because their eyes had been opened by the presence of Christ and by their understanding of Scripture, prayer and ritual.

Another theophany is found in Luke 24 with the disciples on the road to Emmaus. Their eyes too are opened by the presence of Jesus, a fresh understanding of Scripture and the breaking of bread. At its best, liturgical worship does precisely that. It opens our eyes not just that we might experience God in worship but may encounter him in life. Rabbi Lionel Blue exemplifies this when he writes:

> People come and complain 'Rabbi, I went to the synagogue service, I said all the right prayers, I didn't walk out during the sermon and what happened – nothing.' They obviously want to swear at you know Whom, but feel a bit uncertain, and just bottle up their crossness and take it out on their family instead. It happens to me too. I make an appointment to meet God at eleven o'clock on a Saturday morning in such-and-such a place of worship. I arrive early. I say all the right things. I stand up, sit down and stand up again. I bow here, I bow there and bow wow in all the right places, but I don't wow him because He (or She) doesn't show up and I'm left holding a Prayer Book talking to nobody.
>
> Over the years I've got used to God having a will of His own, which I don't understand, and now I wait to see what He does next. I took a service recently, and it was like talking to thin air . . . I went off to meet a friend at Euston station.
>
> By the platforms of Euston I sat down . . . and nearly wept, because to crown it all I was early and the train was late. Some rowdy football supporters were wandering around the station with cans of beer, unsure of them-

selves in a strange city. They knew they weren't wanted. They were defiant and insecure and troublesome. The feeling in the seats was hostile, but the lady next to me looked at them and said, 'Oh, the poor luvs, it's a pity we can't do anything for them.' For them she couldn't but for me she could, because the God I had been hunting through the liturgy peeped out in her compassion. It was our first real meeting that day. In railway stations people are honest . . . and because they are allowed to be themselves God is allowed to be Himself (or, of course, Herself).[14]

Liturgical worship itself can, however, be part of the means by which we are transfigured, for in worship we may encounter the transcendent and immanent God. Worship serves a double purpose. It is the means by which we offer worship to God, but it clearly also has a human aspect. It is both the place of gathering of the believers that they may be nurtured as children of God and also the offering of their lives (as they have been and are) and of their future life (individually and corporately).

It prepares us for life as children of God by informing and challenging our belief system and our own preconceptions. It sets before us the ongoing story of our salvation history, not just as a series of separate events but as a record of God's self-revelation. Similarly, opportunities for prayer and sacrament are opportunities to become aware of being in the presence of God. If the Body of Christ is to be seen in the sacrament, it is also to be seen in our fellow worshippers. To be truly aware of any of these revelations of God is in itself to be opened up to transformation.

To be aware, though, is to cultivate an inner attitude to worship which helps in that awareness. For that awareness to be alive, we need a sense of attentiveness, of expectation, and of generosity. It is this inner attitude which makes of the duty of worship a loving gift to God and to each other.

Moses reveals what it is to be attentive when he approaches the burning bush. He helps us understand that the deepest encounters are not about words, nor even about actions. The deepest encounters are being able to share in another's being simply by being attentive, by being in attendance. Such was the encounter between God and Moses. Moses is attentive to the bush, attentive to the voice, attentive to his own being.

'*Moses, Moses*,' comes the voice from the bush, and Moses dares to listen to a call as gentle as a feather on the breath of God, dares to give it his full attention.[15] '*Here I am*' . . . and somehow his attentive listening allows this encounter with the living God. The 'I am' of Moses meets the 'I AM' of God. There is an encounter of holiness.

To catch a glimpse of that encounter, to see the significance of Moses' placing his whole self before a burning bush, is to fall into a place of silence and wonder. No words can add any meaning. We can only stop and gaze, reminding ourselves of encounters we have had which have led to a sense of being taken out of ourselves into a deeper awareness of that which is holy. How difficult it is to put those experiences into words. It's like trying to describe a piece of music or a picture . . . far easier if you can let other people hear or see for themselves, but even that cannot explain what the original said to you. What could Moses possibly say to his people? . . . 'There was this bush, you see . . .'

He tries something else. He asks for a name. And God gives him two names with a single meaning: 'I AM who I AM' and 'the LORD', both names which derive from a sense of being. Martin Buber translates God's name as 'I am and remain present'.

Here is the fundamental truth that will sustain Moses through the wilderness years, will sound in his ears when the people are murmuring, will call him up the mountain and into the tent of meeting to stand before God who is, and to be attentive to God alone. This is what sustains Moses.

Being attentive to God, then, is a way of living, but one which we bring especially to worship.

We come also with a sense of expectation – the Latin words which begin Psalm 40, *'expectans expectavi'*, are translated, 'I waited patiently for the Lord'. Our expectation may be not so much that we will have an astounding sense of the presence of God every time or indeed any time that we turn up at church, but that our being there will be recognised by God for what it is – our consent to his presence and our consent to be touched and changed by him. The experience of God which we so much desire may or may not happen. With our expectation comes also generosity – a generosity of spirit which is patient in waiting for God but also patient with our fellow worshippers.

This patience and generosity means that we have a much broader vision of worship and play an active part in it – and in particular by relating it to our life and prayer at a deep level. Primarily in worship we shall be seeking God for his sake alone.

We may *look forward* to worship:
- We may choose to pray with the Scriptures of the coming service and make them our own.
- We may become aware of our shortcomings and make confession formally or informally.
- We may become aware of the needs of the world and of our loved ones and bring them to worship.

We may *be present* at worship:
- Not just physically, though sometimes that is all we can offer.
- Present in the sense of being attentive and open.
- Present in the sense of being aware.

We may *carry* our worship into life, letting it have a future dimension:

- Reflecting on those times when God seemed to be speaking to us in worship.
- Praying with words, images or symbols that have spoken to us.
- Praying with our reactions to worship.
- As a result of our prayer, being prepared to make changes in our living, or to be changed by our life.

Worship cannot be seen in isolation from life, and this is perhaps the greatest challenge for the modern Christian, when so often the people with whom we live or work may be a different group of people from those with whom we worship. True worship shows itself outside the confines of church or synagogue. It shows itself in the way we relate to others and especially to those who are in need.[16] When the voice says, 'This is my Son, my chosen; listen to him', God is affirming not only that Jesus is in his image but also that we should listen to him, and in that listening, obedience is also implied. In fact, often the hearing happens as we obey. True worship then includes serving God in daily living. In serving God in our neighbour our need of God's grace is heightened, our resort to prayer is more natural and we are transformed in that double encounter – with our neighbour and with God. It is in this giving of true worth that we approach God in glory wherever he is to be found.

In a sense liturgical worship is part of our waiting on God. It prepares us for encounter. At its best it informs and encourages us so that we are open to the presence of God in everyday life and able to interpret these encounters.

FEAR

If knowing God can be likened to an experience of the sea, then moments of theophany are like being overwhelmed by large and rushing waves. Fear is inevitable – fear of being overwhelmed either by God or by our own sense of worthlessness, fear of the unfamiliar experience and then later, fear of change of perception and fear of changing ways of living. There may also be that fear-like quality of grief.

The fear of being overwhelmed is a fear that many experience not only in the presence of God but often in the presence of the imminent but unknown, whether that be an illness, a changing relationship, a new task or challenge, or death itself. There may even be fear of being afraid when 'the time comes', whatever the time encapsulates.

Fear requires imagination, for fear is often our response to the unknown and to our imagination of what the unknown might be. It is not uncommon for those who are afraid to feel more in control once the cause of their fears is given a name and a more concrete reality. Fear too is not a uni-dimensional response. Fear of death, for instance, may be fear of the end of existence, or fear of being abandoned, of leaving life's work incomplete, of separation from loved ones, of spiritual torment, or of being a burden on others, or not in control of physical functions. Fear is a word which is a crowd rather than an individual. It can crowd in on us.

Fear of being overwhelmed is therefore not surprising, especially in relation to an experience of God. It may produce an incomparable fear as well as awe and reverence and spontaneous adoration. Much will depend on what we know of God before we encounter him in a more astounding way. Fear may be diminished by grace, for 'perfect love casts out fear'.[17] If we have been in a loving relationship with God, as Peter had with Jesus, then our fear is tempered and changed by that love.[18]

Another level of fear is the fear of our own worthlessness. Moments of great joy or love are difficult to enjoy if one has seldom felt oneself truly lovable or worthy of joy. In the face of such feelings what helps us is not looking at ourselves but at God, who sees not us as we are but us transfigured in Christ into what he made us to be, whole and complete. Sustained and sustaining love over years is more likely to reach us than a moment of exultation which lifts us up only soon to dash us down. What reaches beyond our sense of worthlessness is that grace which enables us to begin to trust God's view of us rather than the view which we have absorbed from early and damaging experiences.

Fear of the unknown is a common though complex fear and is eased as we come to know more and discover whether our fear has any real basis. Knowledge often alleviates fear. We may learn not only the true level of danger and risk but also any available means of working to recover the damage.

These are the responses of fear which may assail us through life, but there are deeper fears to do with risking relinquishing our grasp on perception and ways of living in order to take hold of what is our future. Henri Nouwen comes to our aid when he writes of the experience of taking part in a circus trapeze act. If we are to live with our fear we have not to trust ourselves but to 'trust the catcher' – God. Change so often involves a letting go not only of the past but also of former ways of seeing things. Being transfigured by God is at once to be changed and to be the same person you always were. It is the transformation of the imagination and of mind, heart and body. Cyprian Smith writes:

> I am destined for union with God; I was created for that; and will find fulfilment only in that. But I cannot attain this by remaining where I am now; I have to die somehow to the life I am living: so as to find the new life in God. This death and rebirth must involve my *whole* self, not only my daily life, but my thought and speech. No part of me, not even my mind and tongue, can get through to God without passing through the clash of contraries.[19]

It is perhaps this which will enable our learned man to accept being cantor . . . he has not to abolish his fear but offer his fear as well as his singing . . . not to be paralysed by fear but to let the fear itself be transformed by love.

Beyond all these fears, the experience of God may inculcate

a sense of holiness and so lead us to awe and reverence – that fear which is praised in Abraham, a statement of wonder for Jacob, and the beginning of wisdom.[20] It is this fear too that overcomes Peter, James and John. Their tradition knew about the cloud and the glory which it concealed. They were walking not only into the unknown but also into a known God. Their fear is what enables them to walk with full attentiveness and respect. It is a healthy fear, not exclusive of their more human fear, but transfiguring it. Theirs is not the fear of Adam who hid but the fear which draws us nearer to God.

It is a fear redolent with a sense of mystery, attractiveness and adventure, of beauty and delight – a fear which may bring us to worship and to changed lives.

'Be afraid and pray', was the answer of the Rabbi.[21]

Chapter 8

♦

THE PLACE OF ENCOUNTER: TIME AND EXPERIENCE

ON MONDAY, 1 OCTOBER 2001, some three weeks after terrorist suicide hijackers flew into and destroyed the World Trade Centre in New York, Jonathan Sacks, the Chief Rabbi, was giving the BBC Radio 4 'Thought for the Day'. He said this:

> This evening, we begin the Jewish festival of Sukkot, known in English as Tabernacles. It's a simple festival. We take a palm branch, a citron, and some leaves of myrtle and willow, to remind ourselves of nature's powers of survival during the coming dark days of winter. And we sit in a *sukkah*, the tabernacle itself, which is just a shed, a shack, open to the sky, with just a covering of leaves for a roof. It's our annual reminder of how vulnerable life is, how exposed to the elements. And yet we call Sukkot our festival of joy, because sitting there in the cold and the wind, we remember that above us and around us are the sheltering arms of the divine presence. If I were to summarise the message of Sukkot I'd say it's a tutorial in how to live with insecurity and still celebrate life.
>
> And living with insecurity is where we're at right now. In these uncertain days, people have been cancelling

flights, delaying holidays, deciding not to go to theatres and public places. The physical damage of September 11th may be over; but the emotional damage will continue for months, maybe years, to come. Yesterday a newspaper columnist wrote that looking back, future historians will call ours 'the age of anxiety'. How do you live with the fear terror creates?

For our family, it's brought back memories of just over ten years ago. We'd gone to live in Israel for a while before I became Chief Rabbi, to breathe in the inspiration of the holy land and find peace. Instead we found ourselves in the middle of the Gulf War. Thirty-nine times we had to put on our gas masks and take shelter in a sealed room as SCUD missiles rained down. And as the sirens sounded we never knew whether the next missile would contain chemical or biological warheads or whether it would hit us.

It should have been a terrifying time, and it was. But my goodness, it taught me something. I never knew before just how much I loved my wife, and our children. I stopped living for the future and started thanking God for each day. And that's when I learned the meaning of Tabernacles and its message for our time. Life can be full of risk and yet still be a blessing. Faith doesn't mean living with certainty. Faith is the courage to live with uncertainty, knowing that God is with us on that tough but necessary journey to a world that honours life and treasures peace.[1]

For the Chief Rabbi, a 'resonant experience' (i.e. sheltering in a sealed room during the Gulf War) gave meaning to what was already known, and the integration of that experience into life became a resource for the future – 'that's when I learned the meaning of Tabernacles and its message for our time.' The demands of present experience – with all its terror and anxiety – evoked both the memory of *previous* experience (in the Holy Land) and a renewed awareness of the faithfulness of God in the *present* and for the *future* – not only for himself but for others also. For the Chief Rabbi (who undoubtedly knew all the *facts*, historical and otherwise, about the festival), the Feast of Tabernacles took on meaning beyond its 'face value' when he began to see it in the light of his own experience.

For Peter at the Transfiguration, things were not quite so straightforward, and yet he too seems to have seen beyond the 'face value' of the event – even as it occurred – and certainly began to 'make sense of it' in the days, weeks and years ahead. For him, as we have already seen, the Transfiguration was to become an event of enormous impact and influence, taking on profound meaning both for the apostle himself and for the Church.

In this chapter, we explore the Transfiguration as *an event in time that transcends time*. We will look at some of the 'links' which the encounter on Mount Tabor establishes within Israel's history, with the immediate 'present' of Jesus' own journey to Jerusalem, and also the forward dynamic of the Transfiguration as an event which foreshadows the Parousia or 'final revelation' of Christ. We will examine, briefly, some of the fundamental concepts relating to 'time' and 'experience' in this regard (discovering, on the way, how music can help us to uncover some of the richness of these themes).[2] We will try to demonstrate how this examination of the Transfiguration can inform both individuals' and communities' understanding of their own experiences, taking them beyond the mere 'face value' of events to encounter the God of all time and space. Finally, in the light of this, we consider the pastoral task of sometimes being required to enable people to begin to 'make sense' of what happens to them.

AN EVENT IN TIME THAT TRANSCENDS TIME

With the exception of those who, in the past,[3] have suggested that the Transfiguration is merely a piece of symbolic writing, most scholars of the twentieth century would concur that – whether visionary or tangible in nature – the Transfiguration describes an event which took place within the context of *the temporal experience* of the apostles Peter, James and John. In others words, it was something that happened at a particular time in a particular place to particular people. It was a *kairos* event – that is, a 'defining moment' within the *chronos* or ongoing period of time.[4]

Not only that, it was an event which took place in the context of the earthly life of Jesus of Nazareth, Son of God. That this should be so is crucial to the significance which the Transfiguration may hold for mortal human beings, for if the Transfiguration were nothing more than myth, it would remain 'unconnected' to human experience and irrelevant to the truth of the Incarnation. Human flesh and life may be transfigured because, and only because, it has first been transfigured in the person of Jesus of Nazareth, at a particular moment on a particular mountain to the west of Jerusalem.

T. F. Torrance, in his classic book, *Space, Time and Incarnation*,[5] argues that only in and through the temporal and spatial particularity of the incarnation, death and resurrection of Jesus Christ may time and space be redeemed and human beings find new relationship with the God who created them:

> This relation established between God and man (*sic*) in Jesus Christ constitutes Him as *the place* in all space and time where God meets with man in the actualities of his human existence, and man meets with God and knows Him in His own divine Being ... Unless the eternal breaks into the temporal and the boundless being of God breaks into the spiritual existence of man and takes

up dwelling within it, the vertical dimension vanishes out of man's life and becomes quite strange to him – and man loses his place under the sun.[6]

Indeed, it is Jesus Christ alone who gives time its meaning and affirms its goodness, 'through a respectful engagement with creation *including its temporality*, the temporality which was brought into being "in" Christ, "through" him and "for" him (Col. 1:16).'[7]

Jeremy Begbie, in *Theology, Music and Time*, contrasts this positive and all-encompassing understanding of 'redeemed' time with the 'pathologies' of time under the influence of which most human beings exist. He speaks of temporality as having become 'refracted time'[8] – that is, it 'is subject to a disruption between the temporal modes, past, present and future, [and] stands under the shadow of the fall and the promise of redemption.'[9] He suggests that for many of us, the past engenders an acute sense of loss and of the inability of memory to retain an awareness of that which is no more. Even those negative things which *are* remembered (often with a guilty conscience) cannot be 'recovered' sufficiently to be lived again differently. Temporal refraction often also affects the future, evoking either fear of the unknown or unrealistic and unrealisable hopes. And between the two 'lies the seemingly durationless "present", perilously insecure, midway between ungraspable past and unfathomable future.'[10]

Begbie argues that music can offer us 'an impressive resource'[11] in opening up new ways of understanding time and eternity. In his meticulously explained and carefully illustrated text, he shows us how music is made up of multiple layers of metrical waves. Put very simply (and losing the many complex subtleties which he so brilliantly conveys in his book), Begbie demonstrates how each phrase or motif of a piece of music (or metrical wave) cannot exist in isolation from its musical (and temporal) context. Rather, each emerges from what has gone before (even if what has gone before is *silence*) and moves towards what follows, creating tension and resolution at many levels. What appears to form a 'closure' or 'ending' at one level, may be but the beginning of a new metrical wave at another level.

For example, in the nursery rhyme 'Three Blind Mice', each brief phrase bears a particular relation to all the others and to the nursery rhyme as a whole. (You may like to sing it to yourself as you read this!) The first phrase, 'Three blind mice', might be said to be complete in itself, but it leads on to an exact repetition, the two brief phrases making a longer one. A similar musical phrase (at a slightly higher pitch) follows to the words, 'See how they run', which is also then repeated. These four short phrases (or two longer ones) thus become *together* an even longer phrase or 'metrical wave', forming the first part of the nursery rhyme. But it doesn't end there: all that has gone before leads on to the second half of the rhyme; indeed, it is *dependent* upon what comes after: 'They all run after the farmer's wife, who cuts off their tails with a carving knife; Did you ever see such a thing in your life, as three blind mice?' Here, again, there is repetition of a melodic phrase. What is crucial, however (and what creates the sense of forward movement), is the implied harmonic tension created over the course of those three phrases (from 'They all run after . . .' to ' . . . such a thing in your life'), leading ultimately to a reiteration of the very first musical phrase to the same words, 'Three blind mice'. (Although this last repetition is heard *differently* because it occurs at the *end* of the piece rather than at the beginning.)

This very simple illustration will, we hope, enable those who do not have a thorough knowledge of musical theory to engage with the basic principle. As Begbie summarises:

> The crucial point to note is this: however complex the process gets, *one level's return is always another's advance.* However strong closure may be at any one level, *there will always be levels in relation to which closure generates an*

increase in tension, giving rise to a stronger reaching out for resolution. Each fulfilment constitutes an increase in the demand for fulfilment at a higher level. Every return closes *and* opens, completes *and* extends, resolves *and* intensifies.[12]

He applies these insights in fascinating ways to a number of areas of theology, including eschatology and the Eucharist.

Begbie's work may also assist us in approaching the Transfiguration. For when we speak of the Transfiguration as 'an event in time that transcends time', we are alluding to this same sense in which temporality is not simply understood in linear terms (that is, the irretrievable past leads through the durationless present into the unknown future), but one where past, present and future *interweave*, evoking resonance, tension and resolution at multiple levels. More than any other event in the Gospel narrative (save perhaps the birth stories and the Passion), the Transfiguration points forwards and backwards and forwards again in a complex of allusions and characters and symbols through which fulfilment and anticipation intermingle and intertwine, and the glory of the One who was and is and is to come is manifest within the limited particularity of earthly time and space.

For example, the Transfiguration may be thought of as an event which by its very 'shape' not only appears to come to a point of resolution of what has been thus far, but which also anticipates *another* resolution or resolutions (at other metrical levels) yet to come.[13] Thus, the appearance of Christ in glory on Mount Tabor, accompanied by Moses and Elijah, not only points to him as the fulfilment of the Jewish messianic hope, but also *anticipates* the final revelation of Christ in glory at the Parousia. (One might also add that it anticipates the glory of the Cross and the ascent from the mountain at the Ascension as well.)

It is a pattern seen again and again in Scripture, particularly in the prophets. An announcement is made which must be

fulfilled and yet which appears to contradict present experience. Fulfilment comes, and yet only at one level; at other
levels the tension continues; fulfilment (or resolution) comes
later. It is a tension aptly expressed by St Paul:

> I consider that the sufferings of this present time are not
> worth comparing with the glory about to be revealed to
> us ... We know that the whole creation has been
> groaning in labour pains until now; and not only the
> creation, but we ourselves, who have the first fruits of
> the Spirit, groan inwardly while we wait for adoption, the
> redemption of our bodies. For in hope we were saved ...
> (Rom. 8:18, 22–4).

Paul knows that in Christ's death and resurrection all *has been*
redeemed; yet his daily experience of living 'in the flesh' is
at odds with his understanding of life in the Spirit – a life
which he will only fully live when creation itself is 'set free
from its bondage to decay' and obtains 'the freedom of the
glory of the children of God' (Rom. 8:21).

But to return to the Transfiguration ... What *are* the temporal links inherent in this narrative, and how may it justly
be described as 'an event in time that transcends time'? It is
time to examine some of these temporal 'interweavings' more
closely.

MOSES, ELIJAH AND TABERNACLES

> Appearing together with Jesus, Moses and Elijah sum up
> the entire drama of the Old Covenant and point to Jesus
> as its consummator.[14]
>
> *A. M. Hunter*

There can be no doubt that the presence of Moses and Elijah
on the Mountain of Transfiguration is significant. Tradition-
ally, they have been seen to represent respectively 'The Law'
and 'The Prophets' – each strand of the Covenant tradition

finding its fulfilment in the person of Christ the Messiah. Whilst this may be true, it is perhaps too simplistic a view. For here again, there are many 'layers' of meaning, many levels of tension and resolution at work, which relate not only to the *Old* Covenant, but to the course of salvation history in its entirety.

For example, whilst accepted typology does indeed point to Moses as the bearer of the Law, the 'author' of the Torah, the deliverer of the commandments of God to his people Israel, the shepherd of Midian is also the leader of the Exodus, the one who delivers the people from death at the hands of Pharoah. His presence on Tabor points to and acknowledges Jesus Christ not only as 'author' of the New Covenant, the giver of the Law of Love, but also as leader of the *new* exodus – the one whose 'departure'[15] at Jerusalem would bring about the ultimate deliverance from death for all people, for all time – including Moses himself.

Similarly, the one who prayed, 'Show me your glory, I pray',[16] but who had to be content with seeing the 'back' of God as he passed by, had his request fulfilled, not immediately, but hundreds of years later as he stood 'talking with him'[17] at the Transfiguration – itself an anticipation of the seeing 'face to face'[18] that will be the joy of those who are in Christ. It is here that we catch a glimpse of what it means to *participate* in the glory of God. In Exodus, Moses had to hide his face behind a veil after he had spent time with God in the tent of meeting;[19] Moses somehow *reflected* the glory of God after he had been in his presence; but it was a *fading* glory.[20] In Luke's account of the Transfiguration, we read that Moses and Elijah also 'appeared in glory' with Christ – they 'stood in the shadow', as it were, of *his* radiance on the mountain. In 2 Corinthians 3, however, Paul suggests that the transformation is not simply a 'reflection' or 'standing in the shadow' of Christ's glory, but a participation by the Spirit in the transformation – *the transfiguration* – of ourselves into the image of the Lord Jesus Christ from one degree of glory to another.

Thus, in a sense, the fulfilment of Moses' desire to 'see the glory of the Lord' on the Mount of Transfiguration becomes the springboard for the fulfilment of that desire in all who behold his glory and are themselves transfigured by it.

Elijah's presence on the mountain is no less significant. More than a prophet, Elijah had become associated in rabbinic and Jewish apocalyptic literature with the incoming of the messianic age. He was identified as the final precursor of the Messiah, with a mission of restoration,[21] and so it is no surprise to find (hundreds of years after Elijah had been 'swept into heaven' in a chariot of fire[22]) John the Baptist being asked, 'Are you Elijah?'[23] Indeed, Jesus' conversation with his companions on the way down from the mountain also focuses on these two same characters and their significance in relation to each other and to the impending suffering of the Christ.[24]

Yet, Elijah's significance is not and was not limited to the inauguration of the messianic age as understood by the Jewish communities of Jesus' day. Messiah had, indeed, come and his coming was attested to by the presence at the Transfiguration of two of the most significant leaders in the history of the Jewish people. But just as Moses' presence on the mountain was to become a springboard for a deeper understanding of what it means to participate in the glory of God, so Elijah's presence on the mountain was to be taken up by the earliest Christian communities as a springboard for a deeper understanding of the Parousia or final revelation of Christ which they so eagerly awaited. Here again, what was (at one level) *completed* – that is, Elijah's acknowledgement at Tabor of Jesus Christ as the Messiah of God – became (at another level) an anticipation of what was to come – that is, the fulfilment of Christ's messianic calling through his death and resurrection, and the 'completion of all completions' in the restoration of all things in Christ at the Parousia.

The Second Letter of Peter, written to a persecuted and somewhat distracted community, perhaps cites the Transfiguration for this very reason: it is both a foreshadowing of the glory to be revealed, and also an affirmation of the prophetic word which has already been heard. The Old Covenant, and its key figures, bear witness to the supremacy of Christ; its words are valid and worthy of consideration. So the writer looks back in order to encourage others to look forward, and in looking back finds confirmation of what has gone before.[25]

These temporal interweavings made explicit by the presence of Moses and Elijah on the mountain are further emphasised by Peter's extraordinary remark about building booths or tabernacles to contain them. Leaving aside, for the moment, notions of wishing to 'hang on to the moment', this allusion to the Feast of Tabernacles also carries with it suggestions of both *exodus* and *eschaton*, for the Feast looks both backwards and forwards. It was the last of the festivals commanded by the Lord to Moses. It began on the fifteenth day of the seventh month, and it was to be a time of joy and celebration at the gathering in of the harvest.[26] Lasting seven days (with a Sabbath day's rest at either end), the festival was to be a reminder to the people of Israel of their time in the wilderness after their escape from Egypt, and its emphasis was on the *provision* and *presence* of God with his people. It is cited several times in Scripture, notably in the Books of Ezra[27] and Nehemiah[28] at a time when the people have just returned from exile; and again in the minor prophets,[29] where the reinstatement of the festival's celebration is offered as a sign of God's restoration of his people.

Like Elijah, however, by the time of Christ, the Feast of Tabernacles had taken on a *forward* perspective as well and was understood as an anticipation of the time when *all* nations would gather in Jerusalem to keep the festival.[30] In short, it had become a festival which looked forward to the Kingdom of God, and in that respect took on new meaning both for the time of Jesus' earthly ministry and also for the early Church as it looked forward to the coming of that Kingdom in all its fullness. Peter's outburst on Mount Tabor may thus have seemed bizarre at the time, but as he and others reflected on the experience, it was perhaps less so. For the revelation of the glory of Jesus, and his affirmation as Son of God – the one who would restore all people from the exile of sin and death, leading them to worship and bringing them joy and new life – might well be allied in Peter's understanding with the festival which celebrated restoration and worship and the provision and presence of God under the Old Covenant.

Each of these 'Old Testament' features of the Transfiguration narrative – Moses, Elijah and the Feast of Tabernacles – together with the symbols which accompany them (mountain, cloud and voice) holds meaning *beyond* the temporal context in which they first appear and *beyond* the 'face value' of the narrative itself. The links are many and complex, evoking a rich texture of interweaving 'melodies'; some we have heard the like of before, some we shall hear again in a new setting – each significant in itself, yet together producing a glorious and unique polyphony.

JESUS

For Jesus also, we would suggest, the Transfiguration was 'an event in time that transcended time'. In Chapter 10 we shall explore in more depth its place as part of the dynamic sequence of his earthly ministry, looking especially at its relation to his Baptism and Temptation and its affirmation of his messianic calling as the Son of the Father. Suffice it here to say that the one through whom time and space came into being, in choosing to enter into its limitations, experienced on Mount Tabor, *as a human being*, the intersection of the earthly and heavenly – God's eternal glory breaking into the temporality of the world.

In his humanity, Jesus the rabbi would have been as aware as Peter, James and John of the significance of the mountain, the cloud and the voice; he would have recognised all the

dimensions to which we have alluded (and more) of the presence of Moses and Elijah with him on the mountain; he
would have appreciated (and smiled inwardly at) Peter's
bizarre suggestion about building booths. Perhaps his acute
awareness, by the Spirit, of his Father's purposes, meant that
he did not (as his followers did) have to 'make sense' of what
was happening, but as he descended from Tabor to resume
his journey to Jerusalem and his own death, he would surely
have reflected on the experience as they did, and recognised
the multiple connections which it made within the over-
arching purpose of salvation history. It is, of course, impossible to know what was going on for Jesus Christ in the
moment of Transfiguration, and to speculate is futile. And
yet, we must affirm his humanity even in the midst of this
most extraordinary of events, *even as his divine glory is revealed*,
for in that affirmation is the gateway to our own transfiguring.

MAKING SENSE OF EXPERIENCE

Our exploration of the Transfiguration as 'an event in time
that transcends time' has shown how particular experiences
or encounters may take on greater and deeper meaning when
understood within what we might describe as a 'more-than-
linear' temporal framework – one where there are certainly
echoes of and resonance with the *past*, but one also where
those past experiences are imbued with the hope and expectation of what has not yet come to be, and where the known
(but sometimes misunderstood) *present*, and the unknown
future, may give new life and meaning to what has already
taken place. When each new experience is interpreted in this
way, and becomes woven into the 'fabric' or 'music' of our
life and lives together, new possibilities for understanding
may emerge. Such an approach opens the way for connections
to be made, for memories to be acknowledged, for hopes to
be articulated, for present meaning to be sought, if not found.

In its broadest definition, 'experience' is everything that

happens to us, directly or indirectly, that in some way impinges upon our mental, physical, spiritual or emotional being. It may be something we choose or something beyond our control. We may be active in relation to it – seeking, receiving and responding to particular experiences in particular ways. Or we may be passive recipients of it – having to choose how we respond, whether in a creative, destructive or more neutral way. Experience may evoke pleasure, pain, excitement, anxiety or indifference – or any number of other responses. What is clear is that experience and how we interpret it is, in many ways, the 'stuff of life'.

In that we are created with a capacity for experiences that may be identified as of a *spiritual* nature, it is worth asking the question, what do we mean by a *religious* experience? Ninian Smart, writing in the introduction of his book, *The Religious Experience of Mankind* (*sic*), points, interestingly, to the account of the Transfiguration as demonstrating the difference between the 'ordinary' and the 'religious':

> A religious experience involves some kind of 'perception' of the *invisible* world, or involves a perception that some visible person or thing is a manifestation of the invisible world. The ordinary person in Jerusalem who simply saw Jesus walk by was not having a religious experience, but the disciples who saw him transfigured on the mountain *did* have such an experience: the Transfiguration was precisely the manifestation in Jesus' person of the glory of the invisible world.[31]

There are those who would suggest that God's presence in the world and in the creatures he has made means that every experience is *a priori* a religious experience, with the potential to enhance the spiritual dimension of what it means to be human. Nevertheless, many people would want to differentiate between the 'ordinary' and the 'extraordinary' (if not the 'religious') and would do so in terms of whether an experience or encounter may be *rationally* explained. Where it *cannot* be explained, or 'made sense of', it is often relegated – or, in some cases, *elevated* – to the realm of the 'religious', 'spiritual' or even 'mystical'. This is what Ninian Smart seems to be suggesting was the case with the Transfiguration.

Those who are privileged (although they may not always perceive it as such!) with visionary or mystical experience often find it hard to articulate, explain or understand. Julian of Norwich spent twenty years mulling over her 'Revelations of Divine Love' before feeling able to offer any coherent account of what she had seen and what it might mean. That she found the courage to do so in the end is to the enormous benefit of those who read and meditate upon her words. Julian lived in the fourteenth century, a pre-Enlightenment age when 'mystical experience' was an accepted part of life for those so blessed; how much harder it has been for those who have endeavoured to share such experiences since! Even in recent years, where there has been some resurgence of interest and 'belief in' the supernatural, those who see visions and hear voices are still treated with (often unspoken) contempt. One woman had to wait eight years before she found a spiritual director who would accept her description of being filled with the Spirit as more than mere psychological imaginings! For the value we attach to experience in general (and such mystical experience in particular) depends upon the conceptual framework within which we operate. In Chapter 1, we suggested that *spiritual* experiences may be defined as 'those which question our understanding of life and its purpose'.[32] By contrast, a *religious* experience – whilst equally capable of challenging our understanding of life and its purpose – necessarily relates to a specific (even if unconscious or unarticulated) religious framework. Anyone can have a spiritual experience: a religious experience potentially changes the way we live. As Graham Slater has put it:

> Experience is not a simple datum which we report but the result of determining something given in the light of

a conceptual scheme. The validity of experience is thus bound up with the adequacy of the concepts employed . . .[33]

– concepts, it must be said, which have been themselves determined by the particular experiences of those who frame them!

Faith itself is often prompted by some sort of 'religious experience' or encounter, simply because it *cannot* be rationally explained. For faith is nothing less than a willingness to reach out *beyond* what is known, to go *beyond* experience and in so doing to give it meaning and significance. Perhaps it was seeing Jesus Christ transfigured, *with the eyes of faith*, that enabled Peter and his companions to make some sense of the experience in later years. Nevertheless, at the time of the event itself, it is clear that they neither comprehended what was going on, nor were they at liberty to speak of it until after the Resurrection.[34] Years later, however, it had become 'woven into' the fabric of their lives, part of 'who they were', giving depth and significance to their ongoing 'witness to his majesty'.[35]

For most of us, however, making sense of experience is at a much more mundane level. We want to understand why we have not been successful in a job application. We want to make sense of the closure of the village post office and shop. We want to see some purpose in the apparently senseless death of a child. As individuals and communities, we sometimes struggle to see the point of what has happened, and we, like Peter, sometimes reach out for the most unlikely of 'explanations'.

Yet whether the experience is mystical or mundane, the processes of reflection are just as important. And reflection *takes time*. We want to suggest, however, that reflection 'takes time' not only in the sense of the minutes and hours of thinking which are applied to a particular sequence of events, and the internal and external processes to which we subject that experience as we relate it to the concepts and attitudes which we have previously acquired. Rather (and in addition), reflection 'takes time' and gives the particular event or experience *freedom to move within time* – that is, freedom to dialogue with what has gone before *and* what is now *and* what has not yet occurred.[36] In other words, each experience – whether positive or negative or neither – is valued as part of a 'much bigger picture', a 'much longer story', an 'entire piece of music', and as such is neither constrained by, nor required to 'make sense' in, the present moment. To 'take time' in reflection in both of these ways together does not necessarily mean that scales will fall from eyes and everything will be made clear in an instant – far from it! The consequences and meaning of experience may never emerge or be fully understood this side of heaven – 'Now we know only in part...'[37] Yet, what it may do is to allow that *incomprehension* a valid and valued place as the springboard to greater understanding, or (to use our earlier analogy) as the metrical wave that positively creates new tensions seeking resolution in the course of time.

To return to the story with which this chapter began, the terrifying experience of Jonathan Sacks and his family in the holy land during the Gulf War did not, in itself, make sense – 'We'd gone to live in Israel for a while before I became Chief Rabbi, to breathe in the inspiration of the holy land and find peace.' In the event, the experience was a far from peaceful one! Yet it was to teach him three important truths: first, the depth of his love for his wife and children; second, a change of perspective on time – 'I stopped living for the future and started thanking God for each day'; and third, a new recognition of what it *really* means to seek peace – 'Faith is the courage to live with uncertainty, knowing that God is with us on that tough but necessary journey to a world that honours life and treasures peace.' 'Reflection' on experience was thus *carried forward* into the future and, via the BBC, offered as a resource for millions who were, at the time, trying to make sense of the events in New York on 11 September 2001.

This *forward dynamic* is one of the gifts that the story of the Transfiguration has to offer us. For Jesus, it was both about facing suffering as he journeyed onwards to Jerusalem, and about receiving a glory which would be his for all eternity. For the disciples, the Transfiguration only began to make sense much later, but was to become a profound resource both for them and for the Church as a whole. For each of them, it was about going beyond the face value of the event and allowing God, by the Spirit, to use the experience in a creative way – even when that 'way' was to mean pain and suffering as well as strengthening and glory.

Whatever our walk of life, we can often find ourselves helping people to make sense of significant experiences – be they family members, neighbours or work colleagues. We hear the stories of people and groups of people; the significant moments – the births, deaths, marriages, separations, divorces, the house moves, the changes of job, the failures, the successes. We may find ourselves offering praise and encouragement or comfort and compassion, giving advice, or helping to pick up the pieces of shattered lives. Very often what people will be asking (implicitly, at least) is for help in making sense of it all; helping them see where what has happened fits into the 'bigger picture'. In short (though they may not know it), they may be asking us to help give them a different, even 'transcendent' perspective, enabling them to see beyond the face value of the event or the experience itself.

When Job reflected on *his* experience, he was able at the end of his story to look back with a different perspective. Significantly, in the last few chapters of Job we hear of Elihu 'proclaiming God's justice', 'condemning self-righteousness', 'exalting God's goodness' and 'proclaiming God's majesty'. Its effect is to glorify God, and in the light of it all, Job is struck dumb:

See, I am of small account; what shall I answer you? I lay my hand on my mouth. I have spoken once and I will not answer; twice, but will proceed no further (Job 40:4–5).

In the face of God's majesty, Job is enabled to hear the voice of God, falls down in worship and begins to see his own suffering in a different light.

It is when difficult or tragic events occur that people can struggle most to make sense of them, and it is important to emphasise (as we said earlier) that in many instances, 'making sense' of what has happened is neither necessary nor possible. In our next chapter, we shall explore what it means to live with and live through this suffering that 'doesn't make sense'. Nevertheless, we may usefully conclude with an example of how, for one person, the same sort of temporal interweavings, of which we have spoken above in relation to the story of the Transfiguration, enabled him to face his own particular 'way ahead'.

Five days before Christmas, Tony's wife, Sarah, was diagnosed with cancer. The tumour was malignant and would need to be operated on urgently in the New Year. Tony was a church minister. They decided to keep the news to themselves over the Christmas period until things became clearer. They talked a lot to each other and to their grown-up children about what might happen. Tony and Sarah had met at a large city church, where he had been greatly influenced by the minister at the time; indeed, it was partly due to him that Tony had become ordained. They had later been married at this same church and had many fond and significant memories associated with it.

The minister who had been so influential had died just before Christmas (coincidentally on the same day that Sarah's cancer had been diagnosed), and a memorial service was to take place at the end of January, at which Tony was invited to speak. For Tony, the opportunity to return to a place that

107

had meant so much to him and Sarah, and to speak of a person who had been so important in the past came at just the right moment. Although the immediate way ahead was far from easy, the prospect of a return to this 'significant place' reminded him of the many encounters he had had with God in the past, and of God's faithfulness in the present and for whatever future lay ahead for them both. Together, they were able to look beyond the face value of what was happening to them, and recognise that it was part of a much bigger story.

Michael Ramsey concludes that Transfiguration offers a Gospel that

> both transcends the world and speaks to the immediate here-and-now. He who is transfigured is the Son of Man; and, as he discloses on Mount Hermon[38] another world, he reveals that no part of created things and no moment of created time lies outside the power of the Spirit, the Lord, to change from glory into glory.[39]

Chapter 9

THE PLACE OF ENCOUNTER:
SUFFERING

A S WE HAVE NOTED BEFORE, the Transfiguration experience leads to Jesus 'setting his face towards Jerusalem'
and to the experience of his Passion and the ensuing events.
Part of his living out of the Transfiguration was that Passion,
and it is to this darker side that we now turn, and especially
to Gethsemane. At the end of Chapter 7 we returned to the
learned man who was advised by his rabbi to 'Be afraid and
pray.' It is advice which might also be given to the reluctant
Jesus as he enters Gethsemane and approaches his Passion.
His fear reveals itself in anguish as he struggles to offer his
consent to what is to come. In this chapter we contemplate
the times of darkness, struggle and suffering which may be
part of the journey of faith – for Jesus and for us. We ponder
the events of Jesus in Gethsemane and his Passion and Resurrection as a prelude to looking at the hope of healing and
salvation.

GETHSEMANE

If the Transfiguration is a transfiguration of radiant and divine
light, then Gethsemane is a transfiguration of darkness and
is no less potent. It reminds us that our relationship with
God is not made up solely of the day-to-day life of faith. It

also has peak experiences and times of suffering and anguish – times in which, with our consent, God may use our suffering to carve out a space for himself within us. Seen in this context, the darkness is not empty nor our suffering in vain. The darkness, like the cloud on the mountain, talks not of God's absence but of God's hidden presence. As St John writes, 'The light shines in the darkness and the darkness did not overcome it.'[1]

In discussing the Transfiguration, we found that beginning to grasp the symbolic meaning of the setting threw light on our understanding. Gethsemane has its own symbolism – darkness is one symbol of Gethsemane. Other symbols, common to the Synoptic Gospels, include the cup and the garden. It is to these symbols that we now turn.

The darkness/night

In the Christian tradition darkness has often been expressive of the powers of all that is not God – so Jesus speaks of night coming[2] and of those who preferred darkness to light because their deeds were evil.[3] Nicodemus comes by night to Jesus the light, and Judas, going to betray Jesus, goes out into the night.[4] Similarly in Luke's Gospel Jesus goes to his Passion declaring it the hour of the 'powers of darkness'.

Nevertheless, from that same darkness comes the light of Resurrection – 'early on the first day of the week, while it was still dark'.[5]

The night, therefore, can be a fearful place . . . a time when evil lurks and fear marries imagination to threaten us. Night can be the time when fear seeks to overcome faith and we enter a real struggle. In that struggle we may consent to the powers of darkness or we may find God. It is, however, not a struggle of equals, for the darkness cannot overcome even the faintest glimmer of light, but the smallest spark of light dispels darkness.

On a very everyday level, the experience of walking into a

dark night in the country (where there are no street-lights to cloud the darkness) reveals a darkness which, at first, seems absolute. In that darkness we stumble to walk only a small distance. Standing still, though, our eyes become accustomed to the lack of light, our horizon becomes both limited in how far we can see to physically act and unlimited as we gaze at the stars. The initial blindness of the dark gradually gives way to an appreciable change as shapes and shadows become clearer. Darkness limits us and, paradoxically, liberates us. Walking a few yards may seem all but impossible and yet we can see millions of miles and, were we able to read the positions of the stars, we would be able to navigate by them.

Darkness can, however, still be a place of great fear and of immense vulnerability. Those who prefer the deeds of darkness in a symbolic sense are not afraid to use the darkness in a physical sense as a cover. Darkness may also be a time when we are exposed not only to threats from outside ourselves but also to our latent fears which we carry through our lives and which make themselves known when we do not have the emotional energy to hold them back.

Against that recognition of the fear of darkness we may hold all that St John of the Cross and others teach us about darkness – that it can be a place of encounter with God. He assures us that our worst fears need not disintegrate into chaos but that the darkness knows the brooding presence of the Spirit of God, which has a transforming power (the power of true love) to work resurrection out of our passion.

He invites us too to see within ourselves our own transfiguration. In the darkness we may see God sitting in the shadows of our fears and imaginations. In the Orthodox tradition much of the understanding of Transfiguration is about seeing what is already there. For John of the Cross, approaching darkness is both about blindness and seeing. We are blinded by God's proximity rather than by his absence, but if we have faith to wait in the darkness, we may yet see a shadow of his presence beckoning us to new life. As one person said about their own transformation: 'God was a shadow at the back of my mind, one I could ignore for a long time, but which called me to address a particular issue in my life.' John of the Cross, then, sees that God is somehow within the darkness, waiting to pour upon us his healing love.

To emphasise the difficulty of apprehending God in our dark times, we may return to the image of the sea. It is perhaps easier to see the sea when we are not actually in it. Once in the sea, our experience is much less about something other and more about it being the medium in which we live. God may be like the sea . . . we no longer encounter him as different once we live and move and have our being in him . . . he is closer than we imagine.

To enter this dark night of faith, though, is not easy. Indeed, the experience of entering darkness is seldom a choice. What is open to us is not the experience, but our response. Even darkness can be turned to creative use if we respond to our transforming God within and beyond it. Iain Matthew, who has given us so much insight into the life and spirituality of St John of the Cross, writes:

> Night signifies that which comes upon us and takes us out of our own control: it announces that as the place of resurrection.[6]

And in a telling image he says again:

> Night is taking us, then, not to some soiree for a self-preoccupied elite, but to the heart of the world's suffering. It declares the world's wounds to be spaces through which God may graciously enter.[7]

John is not suggesting in any way that because night is a place of encounter and transfiguration we should be happy or content to accept it or even look for it. He knows that to enter the night is to touch on the borders of hell. It is to risk going the ultimate distance from God. In Gethsemane Jesus goes that distance and borders hell in this way – his anguish moving him to sweat resembling drops of blood. John of the Cross does not suggest that all night, all darkness, all suffering is of this nature. But he does suggest that night may be of this kind if our suffering takes us beyond our own resources, if there is a response of faith and if there is an in-flow of God. Of all the accounts of Gethsemane, St Luke's suggests that Jesus' struggle is of this order. Jesus is revealed to be at the limit of his endurance and stripped naked of human strength. Even his friends, though there, have fallen asleep. He consents to the Father and an angel appears to him and gives him strength. God is with him even in his anguish.

The Garden

Jesus' consent, wrung out of his struggle, contrasts sharply with the story of the Garden of Eden where original man and woman seem to struggle little before accepting the snake's kind, if devious, offer of an apple. It is a powerful contrast. Adam and Eve, given each other for company, find themselves naked and immediately cover up. They are afraid, naked, and they hide. Jesus, however, is brought to his garden naked and devoid of all protection. His companions, though present, are asleep. Though afraid, he refuses any way out of his dilemma. Instead he consents to God. Here, in the Garden, Jesus links our creation with our redemption. He reveals, as he does at the Transfiguration, time past, present and future. The symbolism of the Garden takes us even further if we consider the Orthodox tradition. In that tradition the image of the Transfiguration is seen to be one that relates to an understanding of our original beauty:

> He who once spoke through symbols to Moses on Mount Sinai saying, 'I am He who is', was transfigured today upon Mount Tabor before the disciples; and in his own person He showed them the nature of man, arrayed in the original beauty of the image . . .[8]

Thou hast put on Adam entire, O Christ, and changing the nature grown dark in past times, Thou hast filled it with glory and made it godlike by the alteration of Thy form.[9]

In the Transfiguration, then, Christ is not only transfigured himself but we are transfigured. In the same way, through his Passion, death and Resurrection he achieves our resurrection. The same glory is revealed through the Transfiguration as is revealed through the single event which is his death and Resurrection. By it our Adam (or Eve) is transformed into our original beauty – a state we will finally achieve at the end of time in God's presence. As St Bernard writes:

In the first creation you gave me myself.
In the second creation you gave me yourself
And so restored to me the self that I had lost.[10]

The cup

When Jesus prays, 'remove this cup from me', he is clearly asking to be released from the possibility of suffering. He shares our human fear of pain. The cup he envisages is the same cup that he had held only hours before at the supper with his friends. It was the cup that was symbolic of the 'new covenant in my blood',[11] poured out for many,[12] for the forgiveness of sins.[13] This cup clearly relates to the covenant and to sacrifice. By accepting this cup Jesus was seeing his own death to be about reconciled relationships and self-offering . . . for the hoi polloi and for the forgiveness of sins.

Jesus

In reflecting on the symbols of the Transfiguration, we drew upon Abraham Heschel's understanding of symbol to ponder the symbolic power of the figure of Jesus at the Transfiguration. In Gethsemane too there is much to be learnt by pondering the person of Jesus. In seeing him in the Garden as a second Adam we are enabled to see our own story in his. In him we see isolation, struggle and suffering – but all of these being transformed (not avoided) ultimately into glory. In him we see pervasive darkness being experienced and infused with radiant light.

His isolation is important. It characterises human suffering. Even his friends sleep and Jesus is alone with his fears and with his struggle. There are echoes here of Jacob's struggle. Through his struggle Jacob recognises that God is in this place. Through Jesus' struggle we find God not in a place but in a transformed person – and Mary echoes Jacob: 'The Lord is in this place . . . I have seen the Lord.' Iain Matthew comments:

> Jesus wanted, not necessarily to dismiss pain, but to sustain faith in the pain; so John (of the Cross) is aware that one can go through with it, not if suffering is lessened to my threshold, but if I know I am not alone.[14]

But the hard edge of isolation is that we do not know ourselves other than alone. We have then to find other tactics, often beyond articulation. As Jesus faced his darkness and isolation, did he perhaps find within himself a presence of the Father that strengthened him for an instant to say 'yes'? This is no mere hypothetical question, for if this is possible, though not in our control, then it has profound consequences. Etty Hillesum, writing as a Jew from the tragedy of the Second World War, says:

> I know what the remedy is though: just to crouch huddled up on the ground in the corner and listen to what is going on inside me. Thinking gets you nowhere . . . you have to make yourself passive then and just listen . . . re-establish contact with a slice of eternity.[15]

For Jesus, Peter, James and John, this 'slice of eternity' is most clearly identified with Jesus' Baptism and Transfiguration. Did the darkness of Gethsemane take Jesus back to these events and the heavenly voice saying, 'This is my Son, my beloved'? And did there exist in him then *both* rage at the Father but also consent to the Father? Was there both fear and prayer?

Consent to the Father would mean real trust – a trust which means living *as if* he sustains us even when we feel, hear, see nothing. In this trust the presence of God is not necessarily a felt presence but an assurance gained from previous glimpses of the glory of eternity, however simple or dramatic they may have been. To put it another way, what sustains us will be memories of pure love, very human memories which have been recognised and enjoyed as touches of God. In *this* trust, and living as if we are loved, we may discover a new love and a sense of being sustained at depth, though superficially we continue to live with our own Gethsemane. Often this is the point of our own transfiguration ... when we live as if we have moved on in order to move on. Alcoholics and others understand such a way of living as they seek a life of recovery.

Pondering Jesus in Gethsemane and his very real struggle also reminds us that Jesus is on the inside of our suffering and waiting with us to transform it to glory ... not for us in a twinkling of an eye but in that journey of faith which is marked by living and dying and rising again.

DEPTH

This, then, is no superficial approach to suffering. Here we recognise that if the Transfiguration reveals the height of glory, then Gethsemane reveals the depths of glory. The glory is not *in* the suffering but in the God who may reveal himself *through* the suffering, for indeed, 'not every darkness is blessed but every darkness can be turned to blessing'.[16]

The transformation of darkness is often beyond words and

very much in the depths. C. Day Lewis describes it graphically in his poem 'A Hard Frost':

> A frost came in the night and stole my world
> And left this changeling for it – a precocious
> Image of spring, too brilliant to be true:
> White lilac on the windowpane, each grass-blade
> Furred like a catkin, may drift loading the hedge.
> The elms beyond the house are elms no longer
> But blossoms in crystal, stems of the mist
> That hangs yet in the valley below, amorphous
> As the blind tissue whence creation formed.
> The sun looks out, and the fields blaze with diamonds.
> Mockery spring, to lend this bridal gear
> For a few hours to a raw country maid,
> Then leave her all disconsolate with old fairings
> Of aconite and snowdrop! No, not here
> Amid this flounce and filigree of death
> Is the real transformation scene in progress,
> But deep below where frost
> Worrying the stiff clods unclenches their
> Grip on the seed and lets our future breathe.[17]

Indeed, what God does in Christ through Gethsemane, the Passion and the Resurrection is to fulfil that which the Transfiguration promised and which the Second Coming will finally yield – 'he lets our future breathe'.

HEALING

How, then, might any of these insights be revealed in this life for us? We need to look beyond the face value of the events of our lives and see other layers of meaning.

> The mystery of the naked evil of Gethsemane that has its lesser counterparts in every human situation of incurable

illness, impenetrable depression, heartless crime, vicious persecution or cosmic disaster is that it finds its resolution and healing *in the process of life itself* when that life is completely open in childlike trust to the Holy Spirit, the Lord and giver of all life. [Our italics.][18]

In saying this, Martin Israel emphasises that healing is a process and a gift from God. If the death and Resurrection of Christ reveals the transforming power of God, then this paschal mystery lies at the heart of any understanding of healing. Healing is about the power of God to transform us from what we presently seem to be to what we may become in him – which is, paradoxically, more truly ourselves. Healing is, then, not so much about results but about relationship. As the report 'A Time to Heal' explains it:

> Scholars tell us that in Biblical Theology there is a close connection between 'healing', 'salvation' and 'wholeness' ... 'healing' involves a fourfold relationship: to the good earth beneath our feet (our physical environment), to other people (our living and human environment), to ourselves (a right ordering of our inner life), and to God (the source of our being).[19]

Healing is about relationship and above all about a transforming encounter with God. What Jesus makes clear is that to live in relationship with God is to en-flesh the encounter with God which gives us life. It is making real in ourselves what we have heard and seen (1 John 1) and proclaiming it not just by our words but by our changed life. So this transformation will be primarily of ourselves into a fuller humanity. It may involve changed perceptions, understandings and attitudes. There may be physical changes but also changes in our way of living. Often there are changes in our ways of relating to other people, the world and God. Healing has this expansive vision. It is a vision consequent on a glimpse of 'a slice of eternity'. It is a glimpse forward to that time when we know ultimately that we are loved.

The Carthusians are said to say, 'Love has a paschal rhythm', and that takes us into the heart of Jesus' life. Love involves dying and rising, relinquishing and receiving, letting go and moving on. Healing too embraces all of these and has its own rhythm. It is seldom an event but more often a process. It may transform our situation by helping us grow beyond it, or when we have clear limitations it may help us grow within them.

Healing involves transformation at many levels. It is above all about growing into our full humanity, a journey of self-discovery which makes us more available for others and for God. It is a very normal activity – something which happens naturally often without our conscious awareness. A cut finger normally heals itself, the mother or father comforts the child into freedom from fear, and relationships which offer steady accepting love may heal previous wounds. All these healings are very much part of God's gift of healing. They reveal grace-filled transformation to be very much part of God's gift in creation.

They also reveal that much of healing (as well as wounding) happens in very human encounters. Healing itself is as much about community as it is about individuals. Jesus reveals this very clearly as he takes to himself the twelve and sometimes the three (Peter, James and John) into his 'circles of intimacy'.[20] In these small groups of people Jesus grows in self-understanding and love, as do the others. In his early years too Jesus was strengthened through the healing presence of Mary and Joseph, and in their care grew in wisdom and stature as he developed from boy to man, from dependant to adult, from taught to teacher. This 'hidden' healing is immensely powerful in our lives. It overcomes our isolation and gives us the human (as well as the divine) grace to reach beyond what would otherwise be possible.

For Christ, and for us, there is a wider community

represented at the Transfiguration by Moses and Elijah. Our ability to be at peace with those who have gone before us is indeed part of our healing. When their lives affirm us, we can move on . . . loving them still but relinquishing them to God's love.

There is too the reconciliation with God's world . . . and our ability to see God in more and more of his creation. In the light of the world's tragedies, it is not always easy or possible to see the presence of God – any more than it was in Gethsemane – but if we believe in a transforming God, then not only may we live as though God is on the inside of the tragedies, seeking to transform the world's crucifixion into wholeness and new possibilities, but we may align ourselves with his will and play our part more fully.

We may look at the world too in a new light as a result of the Transfiguration. Metropolitan Anthony describes how two icons reveal two very different aspects of it. The first, by Rublev, has a light emanating from the transfigured Christ casting light on everything around. The other, by his master, Theophan the Greek, is much less intense in its colouring, and instead of the transfigured Christ casting light on all else, what happens is that all things gain a transparency. In Jesus' being revealed for who he is, all else is revealed for what it truly is. Sight gives way to insight so that we see not just creation but its life-giving essence – here is a contemplative view of creation which sees a deep-down freshness in all things, as Hopkins would express it. Here the light of Christ does not shine *onto* all else but *from* all else.

Against this hopeful view of the world, however, we recognise the stark reality of its pain as well as its beauty – its Gethsemane as well as its transfiguration. The journey of healing, then, is not easy. It is a journey into truth which will involve the breaking down of all that is not true, a journey into beauty which may reveal ugliness. With Christ we will often come naked before God as we hold the world's suffering before him. Nakedness is uncomfortable. It is easier to dress ourselves in the illusion of comfort and hide in the night rather than be exposed and taught by it. Indeed, as Russ Parker says, healing may be following 'a turbulent way into wholeness'. It is the way of Gethsemane, Cross and Resurrection, the paschal dynamic being an ever-present reality.

And healing will eventually involve death . . . for death too may be the only way of healing. That's not to say that we should find death easy to accept. We may 'rage, rage, against the dying of the light',[21] all our fears being caught up in the primal fear of abandonment and extinction. That may be our most real truth at that stage in our lives – the fear we offer even as we pray. Indeed, our fear may be our prayer . . . our anguish like drops of blood as we walk with Christ the path to glory which can be revealed even through and beyond death.

SUFFERING

None of this is to glorify suffering or death. It is to suggest that God can be glorified through suffering and death[22] and that in his being given glory we may be transformed from glory to glory.

There is a cost in such healing and in such glory – a cost summed up beautifully by Ann Lewin:

> What if pain does not go,
> What then? Scars can be
> Touched to raw response in
> Unexpected moments
> Long after the event which
> Caused them, nerve ends twitch
> Perhaps for ever after
> Amputation.
>
> Healing is not achieved
> Without some cost. It

May not mean the end of
Pain. Healing can hurt
Just like fresh wounds,
As pockets of poison are
lanced, or lesions cut to
Allow more flexibility, For
Healing is not going back
To what one was before,
it is a growing on
To a new stage of being,
through many deaths and
Resurrections being set free.[23]

'For healing is not going back to what one was before, it is a growing on to a new stage of being.' In these words Ann Lewin captures not only the reality of healing but the reality of our transfiguration even through suffering.[24]

Chapter 10

◆

THE PLACE OF ENCOUNTER: OBEDIENCE AND DISCIPLESHIP

'OBEDIENCE' AND 'DISCIPLESHIP' are not everyday words in Western culture. Nor are they concepts (outside a *religious* context, at least) that play a major part in people's thinking. On the contrary, they are often regarded as outdated, oppressive and alien. Little wonder, then, that when 'obedience' and 'discipleship' are mentioned in *religious* circles, they tend to be looked upon with suspicion and mis-understanding (sometimes justifiably, it must be admitted), and those who demand such unquestioning obeisance are regarded as tyrants.

The Transfiguration, however, can open out new poss-ibilities of comprehension, enabling us to recognise the place of obedience and discipleship, not only for our *own* 'living-in-relationship to God', but also their significance for the 'living-in-relationship' of the Son to the Father. For those who were present, and for those with whom they shared their experience, the Transfiguration was to become an event that affected the living of the rest of their lives. In this chapter, we explore why and what that effect might have been, and begin to ask what difference the Transfiguration might make to our own faithful living as followers of and witnesses to the Transfigured One.

'Obedience' is perhaps recognised as something which may

have its place in the family setting – although even that is sometimes questioned – and it still forms a key (though equally questioned) element in the ethos of some professional bodies, such as the armed forces and police. Yet the idea that a person *ought* to do, or say, or behave according to the expressed wishes of somebody else flies in the face of our culture's very strong desire for human rights and personal freedom of expression. We live in a society whose most deeply held values (however misguided) include the autonomy of the great *human* 'I am' – and its implication that 'Therefore I do and say and behave as I choose.' The obvious corollary of one person's freedom of expression and behaviour impinging upon that of the next is less often articulated, as those who devise and maintain the law are quick to point out! At the domestic level, parents of toddlers-to-teenagers may quickly and painfully discover the innate tendency to *disobey* as a far more powerful childhood instinct than that of 'doing as one is told'. Equally, the desire to deviate from expressed orders may never be far from those in the armed services or police, even if the actuality is that most requests are fulfilled.[1]

'Discipleship' is more subtle. Whilst the word is not often used, the concept is not uncommon – although what it means may vary from one context to another. 'Following another', 'being like another' is something most people have done at some stage in their lives. Indeed, the whole thrust and maintenance of the advertising industry – particularly in youth culture – depends on the human capacity to want to be (and to be *seen* to be) like somebody else; to wear the same clothes, have the same mobile, appreciate the same bands. In spite of the autonomy of the great human 'I am', mentioned above, the urge *to be like everybody else* continues to fuel the worlds of fashion, pop, gardening and DIY, to name but a few.

Yet 'discipleship' in our culture is about more than 'following the crowd' and adhering to peer pressure as far as appearances and tastes are concerned. It can also be about 'following a cause', affecting attitudes and values, political stance and ideology. The effectiveness of the Jubilee 2000 debt relief campaign was, and is, dependent on more than a community of goodwill towards the poor; it depends rather on the fact that those who support the campaign believe deeply that the West is unjustifiably taking advantage of the developing world for its own gain and that such exploitation should be stopped. In this case, discipleship means taking action so that those who seek justice not only align themselves with the poor, but also *work together politically* for those countries' freedom from crippling debt.

'Discipleship' comes most closely to a *religious* understanding of the concept when it is about 'following a particular person'. For the teenager, film addict or football fanatic this can simply mean an idolisation of their hero – a form of worship, which finds its outworking in taking every opportunity to see, hear and imitate the one they follow. For the political person, it may mean attending rallies, conferences, campaigning on behalf of a party leader or representative in order to try to ensure their election or position of influence in the political sphere. For the religious person, it may mean dedication and commitment to a particular religious figure or leader and to the teaching they promulgate.

What becomes clear is that 'discipleship' – even in the variety of ways our contemporary culture understands it – is something that demands more than mere verbal assent. It affects the way we live, because it affects who we are as well as what we do. Indeed, the intensity of commitment and dedication of many (particularly younger) people to what they think matters, puts the so-called discipleship of many Christians to shame!

So what can a fresh look at the Transfiguration offer as we explore the theme of obedience and discipleship? Three particular threads emerge for our consideration. In this chapter, we shall explore firstly, the *dynamic nature* of discipleship, what it means to be a 'listening disciple', and the relationship of discipleship to worship. Secondly, we shall look at the *task* of discipleship as we are called to bear faithful witness to what we have 'seen' in the face of Jesus Christ. In our final chapter, we shall move on to consider the *demands* of discipleship – what it may mean to look beyond 'face value', to 'come down from the mountain' and face our 'Jerusalem'. There are, of course, many aspects of discipleship that will remain unexplored: our aim here is simply to highlight those upon which the story of the Transfiguration may have particular light to shed.

THE DYNAMIC NATURE OF DISCIPLESHIP – RESPONDING TO THE ONGOING CALL OF GOD

The first thing to say about the Transfiguration in this regard is that it is not an isolated event. True, it is an extremely *significant* and even *peculiar* event, but it is part of a narrative sequence – part of the bigger story of Jesus' earthly ministry, and part of the ongoing stories of those who followed him. Perhaps this is obvious, but experience demonstrates that more often than not, the Transfiguration (if it is considered at all) is dealt with in isolation from the more familiar, and perhaps more *accessible* elements of the Gospel story which surround it. Indeed, the paucity of literature on this part of the Gospel narrative, and its frequent *absence* in the theological writings on Jesus' life and ministry, indicates that it is often thought to be somehow 'disjointed', 'separate', 'in a different league' from the rest. The result is a discontinuity between the Transfiguration and the events either side of it, and an element of 'interruption' in the stories of the people involved.

For Jesus himself, the events of the Transfiguration take place early on in his final journey to Jerusalem. He has been teaching and healing in Galilee and has travelled north, with his disciples, into the region of Caesarea Philippi. Here, about a week before the Transfiguration, Peter made his astounding declaration that Jesus was the Christ,[2] and Jesus spoke for the first time of his death and Resurrection, and the cost of being his disciple.[3] It is significant that this first prediction of the events of the Passion should have happened *before* the Transfiguration and not after it. Jesus (and indeed, his followers) might have expected the Transfiguration, with its extraordinary, supernatural phenomena, to come first, to be the *defining experience*, the cue for speaking of his impending Passion and indeed, lending weight to the significance of what he was saying. Instead, the Transfiguration is incorporated into a series of events on his journey to Jerusalem. It does, indeed, 'add weight' to the significance of that journey – but it is not the prerequisite of it. Jesus was *already* on the move: he was *already* obedient to the Father and following in his way. Indeed, one might even suggest that it was Caesarea Philippi and *Peter's* affirmation of his identity as the Christ which was the defining moment for Jesus – the point at which he recognised that the time had come to head south for Jerusalem. Here Jesus' self-knowledge is met by (albeit divinely inspired) human knowledge, and it is not until he stands, a week later, on Mount Tabor that this mutual recognition is reaffirmed with the *divine* knowledge as the Father says, a voice through the cloud, 'This is my Son, the Beloved; with him I am well pleased; listen to him!'[4]

There is here, of course, a strong resonance with the Baptism of Jesus. The most obvious is the echo (or near-echo) of the words of the voice from heaven. In Matthew's Gospel, they are almost identical to those at the Transfiguration;[5] in Mark and Luke, the words at the Baptism are addressed directly to Christ – '*You* are my Son, the Beloved; with *you* I am well pleased.' Whilst the voice from heaven in each of these events is significant, the variation in the words would seem to suggest a different purpose for each. At the Baptism of Jesus, it is the Father's affirmation of the Son's identity and calling which is paramount; it is a starting point, a beginning, a 'marker', a call to obedience and discipleship which will find its outworking in three years of teaching and ministry, and ultimately will lead to the Cross. At the Transfiguration, although the words are very similar, the purpose of the voice from heaven is different: true, it serves as an encouragement and *reminder* to Jesus of his messianic calling, but more than that, it articulates and confirms for those who *witness* the Transfiguration, the identity of Jesus Christ as the chosen Messiah of God.[6] The voice is primarily for the *disciples'* benefit rather than Jesus' benefit.

There is an interesting and significant parallel in John's Gospel. In chapter 12 (vv. 27ff), Jesus speaks of his death; his 'hour' has come. He is not on a mountain, and he is not 'in a place apart' from the crowds, and yet there *is* a voice from heaven – heard by some as thunder, by others as the supposed voice of an angel. It is a moment of mutual exchange between Father and Son – 'Father, glorify your name', with the response, 'I have glorified it, and I will glorify it again'[7] – a moment of worship and affirmation, such as is evident in the synoptic accounts of the Baptism. Yet it is also a moment of witness to those around, as at the Transfiguration. Jesus is quite explicit: 'This voice has come for your sake, not for mine.'[8]

Moreover, the voice at the Transfiguration continues: 'Listen to him!' It is not simply a proclamation of who Jesus is, it is a call to obedient discipleship in the context of worship. The glory is revealed. Jesus is identified. A command is given. And it is the coincidence of these three elements which gives the words 'Listen to him!' their unique and life-changing power. There had been many occasions when the disciples had caught a glimpse of the glory of God – in the signs and miracles, the healings, the raisings from the dead, the authority over the elements of nature. There had been many occasions when Jesus had alluded to who he was, made claims as to his identity, spoken of himself as 'I am'. There had been many occasions when the disciples had been astonished at Jesus' teaching, wondering at his words and the authority with which he spoke. Yet not until the Transfiguration had all three elements come together: glory, identification, command – and the impact was immeasurable. It is perhaps *this* aspect more than any other, which identifies the purpose of the voice at the Transfiguration as for the disciples rather than for Jesus himself, for *he* had already assented to the Father's will that he should walk the way of the Cross. His obedience was intrinsic to his identity as the Beloved Son and his discipleship was lived out of an intimate relationship of love and prayer with the Father in the Spirit. For him, a command to 'listen' would be superfluous, for his listening to the Father's heart, knowing the Father's will, was part of who he was. Speaking of his Incarnation, the poet Ben Jonson (1573–1637) put it this way:[9]

> The Father's wisdom willed it so,
> the Son's obedience knew no No,
> both wills were one in stature:
> and as that wisdom hath decreed,
> the Word was now made flesh indeed,
> and took on him our nature . . .

Although it is the most striking, the voice from heaven is not the only resonance between the Transfiguration and the Baptism of Jesus. Three further points should be briefly noted: first, the John the Baptist/Elijah typology; second, the presence (or apparent *absence*) of the Holy Spirit; third, the immediate aftermath of the event.

We already noted, in Chapter 3,[10] the fact that in Orthodox iconography John the Baptist and Elijah are often indistinguishable. In Chapter 8,[11] we underlined the fact that a vision of Elijah might not have been such a surprise for the disciples on Mount Tabor as we might imagine, because of his rich and very pertinent association with the coming of the Messiah. (In addition, we noted the future dimension of this

Elijah typology and an understanding of the Transfiguration as an anticipation of the Parousia.)[12] In the presence of John the Baptist at Jesus' Baptism and the prophet Elijah at his Transfiguration, we have, therefore, a symbolic continuity of the one who announces the coming of the Lord.

A point of significant *discontinuity* between the Baptism of Jesus and his Transfiguration is the presence (or in the case of the latter) the apparent *absence* of the Holy Spirit. In Jesus' Baptism, we read how the heavens opened and the Spirit descended upon Jesus like a dove.[13] Indeed, it is *because* John the Baptist sees the Spirit descending upon Jesus that he is able to identify him as the Son of God.[14] In addition, the Gospel writers affirm that the one who *is baptised by John* will himself baptise with the Holy Spirit and with fire[15] – thus he is both recipient and agent of the Spirit.

In the narrative of the Transfiguration, however, there is no explicit reference to the Holy Spirit at all. Does this mean that the Spirit is *not* present? A closer examination of the event would suggest that the answer to that question is most certainly, no. Michael Ramsey, in his classic text, *The Glory of God and the Transfiguration of Christ*,[16] suggests that the Spirit is manifest in the cloud which descends upon the mountain. In terms of the Old Testament understanding of a cloud as epitomising the presence of *God*, it is natural to assume that God the Holy Spirit is also present; yet, it seems that there is more to be said. True, the Transfiguration is a primarily christological event, but it becomes so *in and through the work of the Holy Spirit*, the one who reveals the Son to the Father and the Father to the Son, and who reveals the glory of Jesus Christ to Elijah, Moses and the disciples. The Spirit's presence may not be articulated in the particular words of the Gospel narrative, but she is most certainly present in the encounters that form that narrative and in the expressed words of identification and command! Only by the Spirit may the Father's words, 'This is my beloved Son; listen to him' be articulated and heard.

The Spirit who descended upon Jesus in his Baptism is, indeed, still present at his Transfiguration. For it is the Spirit who indwells the incarnate Son, who makes it possible for the Son to assent to the way of the Cross, and through whom a foretaste of the glory of the Cross is revealed on Mount Tabor. Like Moses in the Tent of Meeting,[17] that glory shines through Jesus' face as he is transfigured before the disciples, a transfiguration promised *by the same Spirit* in the writings of St Paul to all who have 'turned to the Lord':

> And all of us, with unveiled faces, seeing the glory of the Lord as though reflected in a mirror, are being transformed into the same image from one degree of glory to another; for this comes from the Lord, the Spirit.[18]

The final resonance between the Baptism of Jesus and the Transfiguration that should be noted, is the nature of what followed in the immediate aftermath of each event.

Following his Baptism, Jesus is 'led' ('driven' in Mark) 'by the Spirit' into the wilderness to be tempted by the devil.[19] In a strange way, there are elements in the Temptations of Jesus which are almost a negative image of elements in the Transfiguration.[20] It would be wrong to stretch the inverse parallel too far, yet it is intriguing, for example, that the 'If you are the Son of God' of the Temptations is matched by the 'This is my Beloved Son' of the Transfiguration (as well as the Baptism). Similarly, the 'One does not live by bread alone, but by every word that comes from the mouth of God' is matched by the 'Listen to him' of the voice from the cloud on Mount Tabor. Taking the parallel further, it is surely not insignificant that the earthly glory offered to Jesus in his temptations, as the devil leads him to a very high mountain and shows him all the kingdoms of the world with their splendour, is more than matched by the glory of the Transfiguration itself – also on a very high mountain! There is, perhaps, room for further study here, but we must return to considering the aftermath of these two events.

Following the Transfiguration, Jesus and his companions descend from the mountain and are confronted by the father of a demon-possessed child. The other disciples, who had not accompanied Jesus, have been unable to heal the boy; what follows is another immediate and direct confrontation with evil as the demon is cast out, the boy is healed, and Jesus demonstrates again his unique power over evil. There is no basking in glory for Jesus and his companions; the hard work of discipleship comes quickly back into focus. The journey to Jerusalem must continue.

We have explored Jesus' Baptism and the Transfiguration at some length, because the resonance between these two events underlines the fact that each was significant for Jesus' own discipleship – but they were significant in different ways. The Baptism was, we have suggested, a starting point, a beginning to public ministry, marked out by the giving of the Spirit and the Father's affirmation of the Son's identity and calling. The Transfiguration was a significant event – a 'defining moment' – on the journey, a reminder of the call to obedience and an encouragement to persevere in the face of what was to come; more than that, it was a glorious witness to the Son's identity and a command to his disciples to obey and to follow. The Transfiguration left Peter, James and John (and through their witness, the whole Church of God) in no doubt as to who Jesus was. Yet it was only *one* event on Jesus' journey – a journey ordained before the foundation of the world[21] and lived out in the Son's obedience to the Father in incarnation, redemption, resurrection and exaltation.[22] Nevertheless, it is an integral part of that journey and should be considered as such – not 'left out' as it so often has been, because it is hard to understand.

So much for Jesus himself, but what did the Transfiguration mean for those who witnessed it? What can we learn about the dynamic nature of obedience and discipleship from their point of view?

Just as Jesus himself was already obedient to the Father

and walking in his way, so (at the risk of stating the obvious), on the day of Transfiguration, Peter, James and John were *already* disciples of Jesus. In fact, as the opening verse of each of the synoptic accounts indicates, they consented to Jesus' 'taking them' and 'leading them' up a high mountain.[23] They followed. Their experience that day was, indeed, going to change their lives forever, but it was not the *starting point* of their discipleship; rather it was a defining moment on the way. Their decision to follow Jesus had been made much earlier by a lakeside in Galilee.[24] For Peter, James and John (as for Jesus himself), the Transfiguration was part of an ongoing call to obedient discipleship.

The Transfiguration also demonstrates that struggle and misunderstanding can be part of the significant moments of the journey. Whether inflicted with a natural or a supernatural fatigue after their arduous climb up Mount Tabor, Peter and his companions were 'heavy with sleep'[25] when they witnessed the Transfiguration. It was a struggle to stay with what was going on, but, we read, they 'kept awake, and they saw his glory and the two men who stood with him'.[26] Indeed, as we saw in Chapter 8, Peter could not make sense of what was happening on the mountain, and demonstrated his incomprehension by making the suggestion about building the booths. It did not matter. What *did* matter is that he had grasped the importance of the experience, and responded in a positive, worshipful way: 'Master, it is well that we are here'.[27] He may have got the detail wrong, but he recognised the significance of what was happening, and it changed his life. Perseverance and struggle, incomprehension and yet recognition that what was going on was important: these were the characteristics of Peter, James and John at the Transfiguration, and they were characteristics which were to continue to grow in them and sustain them in their discipleship in the years ahead as they lived out their response to the command from heaven, 'Listen to him'.[28]

An understanding of the dynamic nature of discipleship is

crucial to the life of faith. For Jesus, the Transfiguration resonated with his Baptism, but it was not the same. Equally, it was a foretaste of the glory to come in his passion, resurrection and exaltation, but did not match these things in every detail. As such it was 'woven in' to the pattern of Jesus' discipleship, distinguishable and yet integral to the whole. For Peter, James and John the same was true – reflection on the experience on Tabor both making some sense of what had gone before, and bearing fruit in their witness and in their writings in the years ahead. This is important because it affirms the fact that discipleship is dynamic, that is, it is about the ebb and flow of a relationship with Jesus Christ, and that although certain experiences may play a significant part, they are not the sum total of the journey. To be a disciple is to make a decision to walk in a particular direction – in the way of Christ – but it is not measured by the achievement of particular 'stages' or 'degrees' on that journey. Very often, within that overall dynamic, certain events or patterns may take on a particular significance, but they must be incorporated into the journey as a whole. In this way, they become both a resource and an encouragement – evidence of God's faithfulness in the past and a secure hope for the future.

On the other hand, it can be dangerous when particular events on a disciple's journey are held out as 'decisive' and yet not integrated into the whole. One such possibility is when a person is deemed to have attained a particular 'level' of discipleship or spiritual understanding. For example, classical Pentecostalism will assign great significance to the 'second blessing', the so-called 'infilling' of the Holy Spirit manifest when the disciple speaks in tongues. Important as the receiving of such a gift may be, it tends to 'downgrade' the life and work of the Spirit in the person *prior* to such a 'blessing' and suggests that 'true' discipleship only begins when 'evidence' of the Spirit's work is made known in a particular, supernatural way. It detracts from the value of a person's previous walk with God, even questioning the validity of their baptism and call to discipleship in the first place! It is perhaps significant that as they were coming down from the mountain, Jesus instructed his disciples not to say *anything* about their experience until a later stage, so avoiding both misunderstanding and any danger of 'one-up-manship' amongst the wider community of followers. We do well to remember that *all of us* are being transformed into the image of Christ 'from one degree of glory to another', and the Spirit's work is particular to each person, in each place, in each moment. Those who 'boast' of their experience live dangerously in the life of the Church!

As well as events, for some people, particular places, buildings, spiritual writers or biblical passages become points of resonance – ways in which they are reminded of their initial calling, and encouraged to go on in their journey of faithful, obedient discipleship. For one woman, the words of John 21 were to become a refrain for her journey of discipleship. At different stages, and in different ways, passages from that particular chapter would emerge as significant: the reconciling call to love; the command to teach and care for the flock; the promise of suffering; the temptation to look at others rather than at Christ. Yet each time she returned to that passage, she understood it as an 'anchor', a reassurance – to pursue the earlier analogy – a 'thread' woven into her own story which in different, and often surprising, ways offered security and hope.

For another man, it was important to return from time to time to the place where he had made a first commitment to follow Christ. It was at Lee Abbey, a Christian community and holiday centre in a beautiful corner of the north Devon coast. High on the cliff-top, overlooking the community house and farm, stood three crosses, visible from land and sea. Each year, or whenever he could, he would return to that place to stand at the foot of the cross, to touch it, hold on to it, and in so doing remember his initial 'Yes' to Christ and be encouraged to go on saying 'Yes' in the days ahead. When his teenage son was killed in a car accident, it was to that cross in Devon that he returned to find strength and peace. Indeed, even Jesus knew the importance of returning to significant places when under pressure, as we see in his return to his place of Baptism in John 10:40:

> He went away again across the Jordan to the place where John had been baptising earlier, and he remained there.

Discipleship is ultimately a response to the God whom we worship. It is a response to the glorious 'Yes' of the Son to the Father – his obedience and willingness to walk the way of the Cross. The invitation and command made known at the Transfiguration is to respond to the ongoing call of God, to walk that road in his company and to go on 'listening to him'.

THE TASK OF DISCIPLESHIP – BEARING FAITHFUL WITNESS

We have seen his glory . . .[29]

St John's words from the prologue of his Gospel take on a new depth of meaning when considered in the light of the Transfiguration. John, more perhaps than any other New Testament writer, conveys the enormous importance of the senses in giving substance to his testimony. In the opening of his First Letter, he emphasises the bodily, physical evidence of the Incarnation:

> We declare to you what was from the beginning, what we have heard, what we have seen with our eyes, what we have looked at and touched with our hands, concerning the word of life . . .[30]

And in the first chapter of the Book of Revelation, the vision of Christ's Transfiguration is renewed and expanded as he hears and sees 'one like the Son of Man' whose 'face was like the sun shining with full force'.[31] How surely that vision must have evoked the memory of Mount Tabor! – to the extent that, here also, those who beheld the vision fell at Christ's feet and needed a reassuring touch to help them get up:

> But he placed his right hand on me, saying, 'Do not be afraid . . . '[32]

Physical and visionary, natural and supernatural combine to lend weight to the testimony that follows: John has confidence to say and write what he does because he *knows* what he has seen and heard.

What was true for John was also true for Peter. The early chapters of the Book of Acts reflect an apostle who is unrestrained in his witness to Jesus Christ, a man who cannot but speak of what he has seen and heard.[33] Indeed, although it is very unlikely that Peter wrote his Second Letter, it is clear from what is written that he placed great value on what he had seen at the Transfiguration. His testimony was built on the foundation of his experience both there, on the mountain, and throughout this journey as a disciple in the company of Jesus of Nazareth. When confronted by the need of a community being tossed to and fro by all sorts of dubious myths and stories, Peter resorts to his own vision of the glory of God in Christ to substantiate the truth of what he says:

> For we did not follow cleverly devised myths when we made known to you the power and coming of our Lord Jesus Christ, but we had been eyewitnesses of his majesty. For he received honour and glory from God the Father when that voice was conveyed to him by the Majestic Glory, saying, 'This is my Son, my Beloved, with whom I am well pleased.' We ourselves heard this voice come from heaven, while we were with him on the holy mountain. So we have the prophetic message more fully confirmed.[34]

Many more disciples than those who had been on Mount

Tabor experienced a similar vision of Christ at his Ascension – another occasion when the tangible and visionary, natural and supernatural seemed to combine. Echoes of the Transfiguration are again present – different features in different accounts of the Great Commission and the Ascension: the mountain,[35] the cloud,[36] worship,[37] words of instruction and command,[38] even two unexpected figures also present.[39] Here again, then, there is continuity and discontinuity: sufficient continuity to act as a 'reminder' of Tabor for Peter, James and John; sufficient discontinuity to underline the fact that this was an experience which was building on what had come before, taking them further on in their discipleship, giving them clear instructions as to the way ahead. Confident in their glorified Lord, they await the anointing of the Spirit as they prepare to witness to the good news of Jesus Christ.

Holding on to the vision and taking it with you is part of what discipleship means. Few people today would claim to see visions of Christ, and those that do are often, sadly (though perhaps understandably), treated with suspicion. Despite an increasing awareness of, and seeking after the supernatural, many people still distrust that which cannot be rationally proven – 'visions' and 'voices' included. But a vision need not *necessarily* be supernatural – except in the sense that it may be spiritually inspired. Rather, it can be the drawing together of the hopes and aspirations of real people into the purposes of the Kingdom, so that, in a sense, 'what we have heard, what we have seen with our eyes, what we have looked at and touched with our hands' becomes as important as being 'eyewitnesses of his majesty'. The vision that inspires Christ's disciples today may be as much tangible as visionary, natural as supernatural. So, for example, the experience of visiting the street children of Mexico City can be as much a spur to faithful discipleship as hearing angelic voices in an empty Norfolk church. Similarly, the example of a Christian who works untiringly for the homeless on the streets of London can bear witness to the love of Christ as effectively as being overwhelmed by the Spirit in a charismatic healing service. If a vision of the majestic glory of Christ was the only means to knowing and serving him, Jesus need never have been born, need never have walked the dusty streets of Jerusalem, need never have chosen companions to travel with him, need never have touched and healed and laughed and cried. Transfiguration would have been enough. Instead, he chose both the visionary *and* the tangible, the supernatural *and* the natural: both were part of God's way, and both are part of the calling of those who bear faithful witness to what he has done. When John the Baptist's disciples came to Jesus to ask whether he was the Messiah, he did not blind them with supernatural visions of himself in glory, but told them to tell John what they had seen and heard:

> the blind receive their sight, the lame walk, the lepers are cleansed, the deaf hear, the dead are raised, the poor have good news brought to them.[40]

This 'incarnation of transfiguration' is reminiscent of our earlier comments in respect of icon painting[41] – the icon drawing us in to behold the glory of the transfigured Christ, but *at the same time* transfiguring *us* as we behold him. This 'double dynamic' is beautifully and simply described by Elias Chacour, a Palestinian Israeli, in his book *We Belong to the Land*.[42] Chacour describes how he takes a small group of Palestinians for a picnic on Mount Tabor. He tells them the story of the Transfiguration and encourages them to receive a gift of transfiguration in their daily lives:

> The true beauty of this transfiguration was that the disciples themselves were transfigured. Their eyes were opened to see the reality of their Master, Jesus Christ . . . We also need to have God transfigure not only our eyes, but also our tongues and our hands so that we use them to bless rather than to curse people . . . You all know

about the kind of icon that is painted on wood . . . but I wonder if you know about the other kind of icon . . . The true icon is your neighbour . . . the human being who has been created in the image and with the likeness of God. How beautiful it is when our eyes are transfigured and we see that our neighbour is the icon of God, and that you, and you, and I – we are all icons of God. How serious it is when we hate the image of God, whoever that may be, whether a Jew or a Palestinian . . . We all need to be transfigured so we can recognize the glory of God in one another.

Thus the visionary is 'woven in' to the day-to-day pattern of discipleship, and bearing faithful witness is as much about seeing the glory of God in the faces of his children in need, as it is about seeing the 'glory of God in the face of Jesus Christ'. Both are necessary.

Chapter 11

◆

BEYOND FACE VALUE

OUR EXPLORATION OF THE STORY OF the Transfiguration has led us down many different, yet related paths. We have discovered its neglected place in the history of the Western Church, and its high status for Eastern Orthodoxy. We have endeavoured to enter into the experience of St Peter, and the mystery of St John. We have thought about 'defining moments' and the meaning of encounter – falling in love, growing in relationship, union – and the way in which prayer and reflection can deepen the relationship that may follow. And we have explored our key themes of knowing Christ, worship, time and experience, suffering and discipleship. The Transfiguration has indeed been a rich soil in which to dig.

Yet in the end, more than anything, the Transfiguration is a statement about God in Jesus Christ. Its purpose and value (so insignificant a word!) is in its revelation, by the Spirit, of Jesus Christ as the glorified Son of the Father, in anticipation of his Passion, death and Resurrection, and as a fore-shadowing of his Ascension and Parousia. However much we may want to know what 'actually happened' on Mount Tabor, we are left, open-mouthed, with Peter, James and John, beholding the glorious vision and struggling for words and concepts to explain it.

We don't have to. What we *do* have to do, however, is to

go on asking ourselves what difference *the* Transfiguration and *our* transfiguration may make in our daily living.

One of the great dangers of the Transfiguration story (and a trap which many sermons on the subject fall into) is that the mystical experience remains entirely separate from life.[1] Yes, it may be seen as a resource, a strengthening, something to look back on with wonder – but it seems to have no connection with the ordinary.

The task of this chapter, and of this book as a whole, is to affirm the importance of both. As we said at the conclusion of Chapter 10, the challenge of the Transfiguration is not only how to articulate its wonder and glory, but also how it may become interwoven into the stuff of life. Both the mysterious and the mundane must be held together – the transfiguration of the one becoming the means to the transfiguring of the other. When we begin to look at the Transfiguration in this way, we are expressing our desire to see both beyond the face value of a Gospel story *and* beyond the face value of daily life and its encounters. Instead, we long to see the two conjoin, so 'incarnating' the transfiguring grace of God and espying the mystical in the ordinary. The result is that we behold Christ in our neighbour (and in the world around us), and see faces (both theirs and ours), and all creation, beginning to be changed 'from one degree of glory to another'.

THE DEMANDS OF DISCIPLESHIP – MAKING THE ULTIMATE SACRIFICE

So it is that the test and measure of obedient discipleship is not in the extraordinariness of a visionary experience, but in the 'coming away' from the experience and the way it affects who we are and how we live. Transfiguration is about 'being changed' – being changed *from within* in such a way that we are enabled to face the journey ahead. That inner change may be visible to others (as it was on the Mount of

142

Transfiguration), or it may be an inner change which bears fruit and only becomes visible in the coming away.

One of the ways in which Scripture illustrates such inner change is in the description of the face. Whilst all three synoptic accounts of the Transfiguration refer to the 'whiteness' of Jesus' garments, two also make reference to Jesus' face: 'His face shone like the sun . . .'[2] and 'the appearance of his countenance was altered . . .'[3] Such a description may not strike us as unusual, but in Hebrew thought, it was inconceivable that God should *have* a 'face' which could be seen by mere mortals.[4] Indeed, to depict or even describe the face of God was to be guilty of idolatry.

In the Old Testament, a number of examples may illustrate this fact. For example, after Jacob has wrestled with the 'man' at Peniel, he expresses his amazement that he is still alive:

> So Jacob called the place Peniel, saying, 'For I have seen God face to face, and yet my life is preserved.'[5]

Similarly, Moses discovers that he will not be allowed to see God's face when he intercedes for the Israelites in the wilderness. God will go with his people, and be gracious and merciful towards them on their journey, but his face may not be seen:

> You cannot see my face; for no one shall see me and live.[6]

Instead, Moses would have to be satisfied with seeing God's back from the cleft of a rock. In yet another encounter, this time on Mount Horeb, Elijah meets with God and hears the 'still, small voice', yet is prevented from seeing God's face by deliberately covering his own:

> When Elijah heard it, he wrapped his face in his mantle and went out and stood at the entrance of the cave.[7]

The face of God was not to be seen, nor represented in any way. On the Mount of Transfiguration, however, all this changed. Moses' request was finally granted and he and Elijah talked with Jesus face to face.

Yet it is not only the face of *God* that is affected in encounter: human faces may be changed too. For example, Jacob recognises the 'face of God' in his reconciliation with his brother Esau:

> truly to see your face is like seeing the face of God – since you have received me with such favour.[8]

And Moses' face shines brightly after his meeting with God on the mountain, such that each time he returns to the people after speaking with God, he has to cover his face with a veil because they are afraid.[9] Thus, the face – both God's and ours – can become a means of making visible the glory and work of God within the disciple.

There are numerous examples of this from the history of the Christian faith: the lives of the saints are littered with stories of those whose faces (particularly in their martyrdoms) shine with the glory of God. St Bonaventure's description of St Francis on his death gives us but one such:

> Now the holy Father departed from the shipwreck of this world in the year 1226 of the Lord's Incarnation, on the fourth day of October, at late even of a Saturday, and on the Sunday he was buried. At once the holy man began to shine in the glory of many and great miracles, the light of the divine countenance being uplifted upon him, so that the loftiness of his holiness that, during his life, had been conspicuous to the world for the ruling of men's lives through its ensample of perfect uprightness, was, now that he himself was reigning with Christ, approved from heaven by miracles of divine power, so that belief might be thoroughly confirmed.[10]

Even within the pages of the New Testament, there is evidence of such encounter and change. One such (and one that is particularly interesting in relation to the Transfiguration)

144

is the story of Stephen in Acts 6–8. One of seven 'deacons' chosen from amongst the community of faith, Stephen was recognised to be 'a man full of faith and of the Holy Spirit'.[11] We read that 'he did great wonders and signs among the people'[12] and so provoked the wrath of the local Jewish hierarchy. Unable to confound his wisdom, the leaders of the synagogue stirred up false charges against Stephen and brought him before the council, so giving him the perfect opportunity to preach the good news of Jesus Christ to all who were present. Significantly, all eyes were focused on him intently, because, we read, 'they saw that his face was like the face of an angel'.[13] Here, within weeks of the Ascension and the coming of the Spirit, one of the Transfigured One's disciples bears witness to him, speaking his Lord's words by the Holy Spirit, and reflecting his Lord's glory in his face. And it doesn't stop there. At the end of Stephen's speech to the council, with the leaders of the synagogue enraged at what he has said, one shining face beholds another. We read:

> But filled with the Holy Spirit, he gazed into heaven and saw the glory of God and Jesus, standing at the right hand of God. 'Look,' he said, 'I see the heavens opened and the Son of Man standing at the right hand of God!'[14]

So Stephen dies, giving testimony to a vision of the exalted Christ, not unlike the vision of the transfigured Christ, his obedience to and discipleship of his Lord made complete in the offering of himself, the giving of his life for the sake of the Gospel. In Stephen, the transfiguring glory of God was made visible, and his death became an example to all who came after him – not least to St Paul, who was soon to have his own experience of seeing the glory of God on the road to Damascus.[15]

For Stephen, for Paul, for Peter, James and John and many others, their coming away from an encounter with God, their 'coming down from the mountain' (whether literally or metaphorically), was to mean each facing their own Jerusalem, often bringing with it struggle, persecution and even a violent death. Their obedience was sought, their discipleship and endurance tested to the limit. Yet, even in the midst of such testing, the glory of God, made known in the face of Jesus Christ was to become both their resource and their reward. Perhaps it seems a far cry from our own experience as disciples of the Transfigured One?

Perhaps. And yet for increasing numbers of Christians throughout the world, struggle and persecution are becoming a daily reality. In Indonesia, Pakistan, China, Sudan, Saudi Arabia (to name a few), 'coming down from the mountain' may require a willingness to give up home, family, status and wealth to live a life of poverty, insecurity and oppression in order to bear faithful witness to Christ. Glorious as the vision may be, the reality is struggle, pain and loneliness in the face of evil, and may even lead to the ultimate sacrifice of one's life. Christians in the West would do well to shake off their complacency in this regard and pray both for their brothers and sisters elsewhere, and also for a renewed vision to equip them for the severe demands of discipleship which may lie ahead.

For most of us, however, both the vision and the demand are more muted. The change is both more gradual and less visible – it is a change *within*. It is the transfiguration that comes less often through glorious visions on mountaintops than through the faithful and prayerful living out of our discipleship from day to day. There will be moments when we 'see' the face of Christ in our brother or sister – and our heart will be 'strangely warmed'. One woman described such an experience in this way:

> I really wasn't sure that my sister should be ordained priest. It seemed such a big step for her and her family, and I was unconvinced that it was theologically 'right' in any case. When the time came for the ordination, I went to the service – somewhat reluctantly it has to be

said. But once I was there, all my doubts disappeared, for as the moment came for the laying on of hands, the sun suddenly streamed through the cathedral clerestory window and alighted on her face as she knelt before the bishop. It was an amazing and unforgettable moment – and I knew in that instant that, despite all my misgivings, it was indeed right for her to be ordained.

More often, faithful discipleship will be about being willing to return to the mountain at every opportunity in worship, in adoration, in prayer, gazing at the Transfigured One and then coming down the mountain to the rough and tumble of a needy world – *holding the vision within*. As we do, we walk our path in identification with Jesus on his journey to Jerusalem, strengthened in his company as we face our own. Michael Ramsey draws the double dynamic together when he says:

> The vision of Christ is the transfiguration of man (*sic*) . . . the Christian life is a rhythm of going and coming; and the gospel narrative of the ascent of Hermon,[16] the metamorphosis and the descent to the faithless and perverse generation is a symbol of the mission of the Church in its relation to the world.[17]

RAPHAEL'S *TRANSFIGURATION* – GLORY AND REALITY TOGETHER

This sense of 'going and coming', this 'ascent and descent', is vividly depicted in Raphael's painting, the full title of which is *Transfiguration and the Failure to Heal*.[18] It was his final work, commissioned by Cardinal Giulio de Medici and painted between 1518 and 1520. It is believed to have been unfinished on his death on Good Friday, 6 April 1520, and was completed by one of his students. The painting is unique amongst Western depictions of the Transfiguration (of which there are numerous examples up until the eighteenth century –

although it became less popular a subject after the Council of Trent [1537 onwards]), in that it shows not only Christ in glory on the mountain, but also the encounter between the disciples and the father of the demon-possessed boy in the foreground.

Although in the Gospel the healing of the boy follows the Transfiguration, Raphael joins them at one point in time. Glory and failure, the heavenly and the earthly, the mysterious and the mundane, are presented in close juxtaposition on the same canvas. The drama of the transfigured Christ, in white robes, against an even whiter light emanating from behind him dominates the upper half of the painting; a different drama takes place below, as the impotent disciples fail to cure the sick child. The two parts of the canvas are linked by the uplifted arms of two of the apostles and the child himself, drawing the eye to the vision of the Saviour who alone can bring healing and salvation. At the same time, other arms point towards the child, and away from the canvas towards the one who views the painting, inviting the onlooker also to enter into the ordinariness and the glory which this work of art so stunningly and simultaneously portrays.

There are some 25 figures in the painting, each with a face. Some are completely hidden, some more obscure than others. One of the disciples on the mountain buries his head in his hands; the other two shade their eyes from the blinding light. Moses and Elijah are seen in profile, whilst the face of Christ is surprisingly feminine and effete.

It is the faces in the lower half of the painting, however, that express the depth and variety of feelings of the characters in this painting. Here, amongst the disciples, there is concern and compassion for the child and his father, but also questioning, incomprehension and disappointment. Those who accompany the epileptic child express hope, longing, and – again – incomprehension at the inability of the disciples to heal, when the one they follow so evidently exudes power and glory beyond measure.

Transfiguration by Raphael (1483–1520), Vaticano Pinacoteca.
Photograph courtesy of Scala Group.

Where is the connection? What has the Transfiguration of Christ to say to the pain of an unhealed child and a disillusioned community?

In a coalescence of the two images on the one canvas, Raphael forces us to encounter both realities. We can neither live only on the mountain, escaping into our comfortable 'booths', capturing the moment, relishing the mystery; nor can we live only in the valley, faced with human pain, a community's demands and our own impotence. We need both, and God in his grace, allows us to *experience* both – to encounter him *in* both, and be transfigured *by* both.

So often, we live for the transfiguring experiences and end up dying from day to day. We look to the retreats, the quiet days, the conventions, the conferences, to 'recharge our batteries', to experience a 'spiritual high', only to come back down to earth with a bump when the silence has been broken, the echo of the choruses has disappeared and the speakers' words have faded from our memories. There is a place and time for such things. Yet, we also need to allow God to open our eyes to the wonder and awe of seeing his face reflected and shining in the ordinary, the mundane and the suffering, as it is transfigured by his grace, revealing his glory in the world. For when we do, every encounter may be a transfiguring encounter through which Christ is made known.

To live in this way transforms discipleship. Sight gives way to insight, worship becomes response, reflection and hope is interwoven with experience and suffering may be a means by which we grow in glory. No longer is discipleship a case of 'matching up' to the performance of other disciples or even trying (by our own efforts) to imitate Christ himself. Discipleship is not the imitation of a life, but rather the transformation by a life and a living of a life. That transformation by Christ is the work of the Spirit, changing us from one degree of glory to another. The invitation is both to ascend the mountain and descend from it again – to see the vision and listen to the voice, and then see and hear the same Transfigured One in the faces and in the voices of his children. It is when disciples live in this way that we truly begin to see beyond face value and encounter God.

◆

NOTES

1: LOOKING BEYOND THE INTRODUCTION

1. Michel Quoist, *Prayers of Life* (Dublin, Gill and Macmillan, 1963), p. 23f.
2. Julian of Vezelay quoted in Robert Atwell, *Celebrating the Seasons* (Norwich, Canterbury Press, 1999), p. 45.
3. Gary Ansdell, *Music for Life* (London, Kingsley, 1995), p. 63.
4. Monica Furlong, *Travelling In*, quoted in *The Easter Spirit* (London, DLT, 1990), p. 118f.
5. We may define spiritual experiences as those which question our understanding of life and its purpose. Spiritual experiences therefore raise issues of meaning and are open to all. Religious experiences are those which relate to a specific religious framework of understanding. Equally they may challenge our understanding and the meaning we give to events and experiences.
6. Ed. Michael Glazier & Monika K. Hellwig, *The Modern Catholic Encyclopaedia*, pp. 78–9.
7. John McCarthy and Jill Morrell, *Some Other Rainbow* (London, Bantam Press, 1993), p. 66.
8. Revd Graham Slater in *The Expository Times*, Vol. 113, No. 2 (Edinburgh, T & T Clark, November 2001), p. 59.
9. Cf. Vanessa Herrick and Ivan Mann, *Jesus Wept* (London, DLT, 1998), p. 91.
10. Richard Rhodes, *The Making of the Atomic Bomb* (New York, Touchstone, 1988), p. 3.
11. Ibid., p. 28.
12. C. Day Lewis, *The Complete Poems* (London, Sinclair-Stevenson, 1992), p. 684.

2: A FORGOTTEN FEAST

1. Kenneth E. Kirk, in *The Vision of God* (London, Longman, Green & Co., 1931): 'Before the earliest gospel had assumed its present shape, the Church had fixed upon the Transfiguration as the central moment of the Lord's earthly life.'
2. This significance – particularly in relation to the Parousia, will be explored in greater detail below.
3. Origen (AD 231–54): 'Thabor is the mountain of Galilee on which Christ was transfigured' – from commentary on Psalm 88:13.
4. Catechesis II.16.
5. From Jerome's letters: Ep. xlvi, ad Marcel; Ep. viii, ad Paulin.; Ep. Cviii, ad Eust.
6. See article by F. G. Holweck in *Catholic Encyclopedia* (downloaded from entry on 'Feast of the Transfiguration of Christ', www.newadvent.org).
7. There is some evidence of a fourth-century church dedicated to the Transfiguration on Mount Tabor. See Marshall, *The Transfiguration of Jesus* (London, DLT, 1994), ch. 1.
8. Ibid.
9. It is now a festival on a par with the commemoration of the apostles and the lesser feasts of the Blessed Virgin Mary.
10. See also Ch. 9, p. 120.
11. A. M. Ramsey, *The Glory of God and the Transfiguration of Christ* (London, Longman, Green & Co., 1949), p. 135.
12. See, for example, Ware on the Hesychastic controversy in *The Orthodox Church* (Harmondsworth, Penguin, 1963), pp. 70ff.
13. Stephen C. Barton, 'The Transfiguration of Christ according to Mark and Matthew: Christology and Anthropology', in *'Auferstehung – Resurrection' – 4th Durham-Tubingen Research Symposium – Resurrection, Transfiguration and Exaltation in Old Testament, Ancient Judaism and Early Christianity* (Mohr Siebeck, Tubingen, 2001), pp. 231–46.
14. Edinburgh, T & T Clark, 1942, ch. 1.
15. Ramsey, 1949, op. cit., ch. 10.
16. Cf. Riesenfeld in *Jésus transfiguré* (1947), who attempts to relate the Transfiguration to the enthronement tradition of the Jewish cultus (cf. Mowinckel's work on the Psalms).
17. Boobyer, *St Mark and the Transfiguration Story* (Edinburgh, T & T Clark, 1942), pp. 6ff.
18. E.g. Wellhausen, Goetz.
19. E.g. 'The Mystic Way' (1913) in *Mysticism: The nature and development of spiritual consciousness* (Oxford, Oneworld Publications, 1993) and *Worship* (London, Nisbet & Co., 1936).

3: THROUGH THE EYES OF PETER

1. For a fuller summary treatment of each Gospel, see Marshall, 1994, op. cit.

2. Cf. Isa. 60:1 and Westerman's comment concerning the word 'shine'. He says, 'What the prophet has in mind is the beaming look on the face'. Claus Westerman, *Isaiah 40 – 66: a commentary* (London, SCM Press, 1966), p. 357.
3. Mark 8:27ff; Matt. 16:13ff; Luke 9:18ff.
4. Stephen Barton identifies a threefold pattern in this episode (and in Mark's Gospel as a whole) which may usefully be applied to the Transfiguration account also. The pattern is as follows: (i) Christological disclosure focusing on the Messiah as the suffering and vindicated Son of Man; (ii) misunderstanding of this revelation by the disciples or their representatives; (iii) instruction about discipleship. See Barton, 2001, op. cit., pp. 234–5.
5. Marshall, 1994, op. cit., p. 39.
6. 'I do not know the man!' (Matt. 26:74).
7. Cf. 2 Pet. 1:15–18.
8. Exod. 24; 34; 1 Kings 18.
9. Luke 6:12.
10. Matt. 4:8.
11. Matt. 18:16.
12. Cf. Acts 1:11.
13. See Philip Yancey, *The Jesus I Never Knew* (London, Marshall Pickering, 1995), p. 74.
14. και εγενετο εν τω προσευχεσθαι αυτον το ειδος του προσωπου αυτου ετερον . . . (*kai egeneto proseuxesthai to eidos tou prosopou auto heteron* . . .).
15. Matthew and Mark: και μετεμορφωθη εμπροσθεν αυτων (*kai metemorphothe hemprosthen auton*).
16. Cf. Exod. 13:21; 19:16ff.
17. Cf. 1 Thess. 4:16–17.
18. Matt. 17:9–13; Mark 9:9–13; cf. John 1:21, 25. Interestingly, in Orthodox iconography Elijah and John the Baptist are often indistinguishable.
19. See Lev. 23:33–43.
20. For further study see commentaries by Bauckham (1983), Hillyer (1995), Knight (1995).
21. The word used here is εξοδον (*exodon*). (The only other place where it occurs in the NT is in 2 Pet. 15, where 'pseudo' Peter is speaking of his impending death.) 'Just as the escape of Israel from the hands of Pharoah meant the safe delivery of God's chosen people, so the death of Jesus in the holy city would lead to people being delivered from the sin that had imprisoned them' (Marshall, 1994, op. cit., p. 59).
22. There would seem to be a particular connection between those who experience 'mystical revelation' of one sort or another, also being called to suffer for the sake of Christ, e.g. St Francis, Julian of Norwich, St Ignatius, to name but three.
23. Matthew adds the words, 'with whom I am well pleased', cf. the baptism in Matt. 3:17.

24. Mark 1:17; Matt. 4:19; cf. Luke 5:11.
25. John 21:19.
26. Barton, 2001, op. cit., p. 246.

4: I HAVE SEEN THE LORD

1. John 8:56–8.
2. Lev. 24:16.
3. The falling to the ground finds parallels in Matthew's account of the Transfiguration (Matt. 17:6).
4. E.g. Gen. 15:1, 26:24, etc. See also Luke 1:26–38.
5. The bread of life, John 6:35, 38; the light of the world, 8:12; 9:5; the gate for the sheep, 10:7, 9; the good shepherd, 10:11, 14; the resurrection and the life, 11:25; the way, the truth and the life, 14:6; the vine, 15:1, 5.
6. Isa. 43:25.
7. *The Way,* Supplement No. 94 (London, The Way Publications, 1999/94).
8. John 1:16–17.
9. See also the song in Exod. 15, after the crossing of the Red Sea.
10. R. E. Brown, *The Gospel According to St John: Vol. 1* (London, Geoffrey Chapman, 1966), p. 527.
11. John 5:46; 1:17.
12. John 2:11; 20:30f.
13. Changing water into wine (John 2:1–11); curing of the official's son (4:46–54); curing of the paralytic (5:1–15); multiplication of the loaves (6:1–15); walking on the sea (6:16–21); curing of the blind man (ch. 9); raising of Lazarus (ch. 11).
14. John 14:9.
15. John 5:19.
16. John 1:10–13 etc.
17. See Ch. 6.
18. See, e.g., John 12:38ff.
19. John 2:23–5; 3:2–3; 4:45–8 etc. and see R. E. Brown, 1966, op. cit., p. 531.
20. John 2:1–11.
21. John 17:24; 20:29.
22. Deut. 34:10ff; John 20:30f.
23. See, e.g., Deut. 29:2–4; John 12:38 etc.
24. John 4:25.
25. John 4:23.
26. D. S. Russell, *The Method and Message of Jewish Apocalyptic 200 BC to 100 AD* (London, SCM, 1964), pp. 137f.
27. John 3:35.
28. John 5:43; 17:11.
29. John 10:25.
30. John 1:12; 3:18.
31. John 14:13; 15:16; 16:23, 26.
32. John 15:21; 17:11.

33. John 1:12.
34. Johs Pedersen, *Israel: Its Life and Culture* (London, Geoffrey Cimberledge, 1926), p. 245.
35. John 3:35; 5:20.
36. John 17:5, 24.
37. John 1:39.
38. John 17:3.
39. John 6:42.
40. John 2:24; 4:29, 39; 5:42; 6:64 etc.
41. John 6:42; 7:27; 8:19, 54.
42. John 10:14; 14:7, 17.
43. John 14:20.
44. Mark 8:27ff; Luke 9:18ff etc.
45. Luke 9:51.
46. John 12:24.
47. John 21:17.
48. John 20:29.
49. John 3:8; 20:22.
50. John 16:13 etc.
51. John 9:38; 11:32.
52. 1 John 4:18.
53. E.g. Exod. 16:10; 24:17.
54. R. E. Brown, 1966, op. cit., p. 503.
55. John 12.
56. John 16:1; 17:17f; 12:26.
57. John 21:18f.
58. Ramsey, 1949, op. cit., p. 72.
59. John 17:26.
60. John 1:18.
61. John 13:36f.
62. John 17:5.

5: GOD IN THE PLACE OF ENCOUNTER

1. St Anselm, *Proslogion*. See also Chs. 8 and 11 of this book regarding the desire to see God's face.
2. Further source unknown.
3. Gonville ffrench-Beytagh, *Encountering Light* (Glasgow, Collins, 1975), pp. 8f.
4. Isa. 6.
5. Sebastian Faulks, *On Green Dolphin Street* (London, Hutchinson, 2001), p. 297.
6. Mark 8.
7. Louis J. Puhl SJ, *The Spiritual Exercises of St Ignatius* (Chicago, Loyola University Press, 1951), p. 12.
8. See p. 43.

9. See, for instance, Robert Davis, *My Journey into Alzheimer's Disease* (Illinois, Tyndale House, 1989).
10. Charles de Foucauld (1858–1916).
11. George Aschenbrenner, *The Way* Supplement No. 52 (London, The Way Publications, 1985), p. 40.
12. Abraham Heschel, *Man's Quest for God* (Santa Fe, Aurora Press, 1998), p. 114.
13. Ibid., p. 89.
14. John of Damascus in Timothy Ware, *The Orthodox Church* (Harmondsworth, Penguin, 1984), p. 73.
15. Anonymous.
16. Russ Parker, *Healing Wounded History* (London, DLT, 2001), p. 4.
17. St Irenaeus, 'Against all heresies' in Robert Atwell, 1999, op. cit., p. 412.

6: THE PLACE OF ENCOUNTER: KNOWING CHRIST

1. See, e.g., Deut. 4:39–46; 29:2–6; Isa. 43:10; Hos. 6:6; Ps. 46:10.
2. Insight, as we have said earlier, requires this element of learning as a necessary part of interpretation.
3. Deut. 1:31.
4. Deut. 6:4; 7:8.
5. Gen. 8:11.
6. Trans. Clifton Walters, *The Cloud of Unknowing and other works* (Harmondsworth, Penguin Classics, 1978), p. 115.
7. John 17:1–3; 1 Cor. 15:43; 2 Cor. 3:18.
8. Phil. 3:8.
9. Cf. Ch. 3, p. 21.
10. Teilhard de Chardin, quoted in Margaret Guenther *Holy Listening* (London, DLT, 1992), p. 82.
11. See Ch. 3, p. 21.
12. Cf. J. V. Taylor, *The Christlike God* (London, SCM, 1992), pp. 35–9.
13. Patrick Hart & Jonathan Montaldo (eds.), *The Intimate Merton: His life from His Journals* (Oxford, Lion, 2000), p. 284.
14. Martin Thornton, *My God* (London, Hodder & Stoughton, 1974), pp. 181f.
15. Ann Lewin, *Candles and Kingfishers* (Peterborough, Foundery Press, 1997), p. 64. We are grateful to Ann Lewin and to the Methodist Publishing House for permission to quote from this publication.
16. Martin Thornton, *My God*, p. 34.
17. See John 5:39.
18. N.B.: 'The purpose of the Eucharist is not to change bread and wine, but to change you and me.' Robert Taft sj, *Liturgy of the Hours in East and West: The Origins of the Divine Office and its meaning for today* (Collegeville, Minnesota, 1986), p. 360.
19. Mark 8:29.
20. Ann Lewin, *Candles and Kingfishers*, p. 21

21. Luke 15:32ff.
22. Gerald C. May, *Addiction and Grace* (San Francisco, Harper & Row, 1988), p. 4.
23. Ibid., p. 18.

7: THE PLACE OF ENCOUNTER: WORSHIP AND FEAR

1. Heschel, 1998, op. cit., p. 89.
2. See also Ch. 3.
3. Gen. 22.
4. Ps. 121.
5. See Deut. 12:2.
6. Exod. 20:21.
7. A. Michael Ramsey, 1949, op. cit., p. 17.
8. Ezek. 1:28; Dan. 8:17; 10:9 etc.
9. Heschel, 1998, op. cit., pp. 120–24.
10. Job 42:5–6.
11. Isa. 6:5.
12. Ezek. 36.
13. Luke 5:8.
14. Lionel Blue, quoted in Ivan Mann, *The Golden Key* (Northampton, MNDA, 1990), p. 29.
15. Exod. 3.
16. See, e.g., Isa. 1:10–18, 58.
17. 1 John 4:18.
18. John 21:15–19.
19. Cyprian Smith, *The Way of Paradox* (London, DLT, 1987), p. 27.
20. Gen. 22:12; 28:17; Prov. 1:7.
21. Heschel, 1998, op. cit., p. 89.

8: THE PLACE OF ENCOUNTER: TIME AND EXPERIENCE

1. © 2001 BBC. Rabbi Jonathan Sacks, 'Thought for the Day', BBC Radio 4 *Today* programme, 1 October 2001. Used by permission.
2. We are particularly indebted to Jeremy Begbie for his innovative work in this area. See Jeremy S. Begbie, *Theology, Music and Time* (Cambridge, Cambridge University Press, 2000).
3. See Ch. 2, p. 16.
4. For more on *kairos* and *chronos* see, for example, respective entries in *Theological Dictionary of the New Testament*, Vol. III (ed. G. Kittel), pp. 455ff, and Vol. IX (eds. G. Kittel & G. Friedrich), pp. 581ff (Grand Rapids, Michigan, Eerdmanns, 1965 and 1974).
5. Edinburgh, T & T Clark, 1997.
6. Ibid., pp. 75–6.
7. Begbie, 2000, op. cit., p. 147.
8. Ibid., pp. 147ff.
9. Ibid., p. 147.

10. Ibid., p. 148.
11. Ibid., p. 154.
12. Ibid., p. 107. Those who wish to explore these ideas further should read especially chs. 2 and 3 of *Theology, Music and Time*.
13. Cf. Begbie's idea of 'a prefigured ending', Begbie, 2000, op. cit., pp. 111f.
14. A. M. Hunter, *The Work and Words of Jesus* (London, SCM Press, 1973), p. 66.
15. Luke 9:31: οι οφθεντες εν δοξη ελεγον την εξοδον αυτου, ην ημελλεν πληρουν εν Ιερουσαλημ 'They appeared in glory and were speaking of his *departure*, which he was about to accomplish at Jerusalem.'
16. Exod. 33:18.
17. Matt. 17:3; cf. Exod. 33:11.
18. 1 Cor. 13:12; cf. 2 Cor. 3:18.
19. Exod. 34:34–5.
20. Cf. 2 Cor. 3:7ff.
21. See Ramsey, 1949, op. cit., p. 114.
22. 2 Kings 2:11; cf. 1 Thess. 4:17.
23. John 1:21.
24. Matt. 17:10–13; Mark 9:11–13.
25. 2 Pet. 1:19, 'So we have the prophetic message more fully confirmed . . . '
26. See Lev. 23:33–43.
27. Ezra 3:4.
28. Neh. 8:14–17.
29. Hos. 12:9.
30. Zech. 14:16.
31. N. Smart, *The Religious Experience of Mankind* (London, Collins/Fontana, 1971), p. 28.
32. See Ch. 1, p. 5ff and n5.
33. Graham Slater, 'Experience' in *Dictionary of Spirituality*, ed. Gordon S. Wakefield (London, SCM Press, 1983).
34. Matt. 17:9; Mark 9:9; Luke 9:36.
35. 2 Pet. 1:17; cf. John 1:14.
36. It is worth saying that *reflection* (in the terms which we are suggesting) is, perhaps, an inadequate term, in that it inherently seems to suggest a 'looking back' to previous experience, rather than the more open-ended view we are advocating.
37. 1 Cor. 13:12.
38. Or Tabor.
39. Ramsey, 1949, op. cit., p. 147.

9: THE PLACE OF ENCOUNTER: SUFFERING
1. John 1:5.
2. John 11:4.
3. John 3:19.
4. John 13:30.

5. John 20:1.
6. Iain Matthew, *The Impact of God* (London, Hodder and Stoughton, 1995), p. 55.
7. Ibid., p. 57.
8. Trans. Mother Mary, *The Festal Menaion* (London, Faber & Faber, 1969), p. 476.
9. Ibid., p. 482.
10. St Bernard.
11. Luke 22:20.
12. Mark 14:22.
13. Matt. 26:28.
14. Iain Matthew, 1995, op. cit., p. 115.
15. Etty Hillesum, *An Interrupted Life* (Washington, Washington Square Press, 1983), pp. 46f.
16. Iain Matthew, 1995, op. cit., p. 141.
17. C. Day Lewis, *The Complete Poems* (London, Sinclair-Stevenson, 1992), p. 393.
18. Martin Israel, *Gethsemane* (London, Fount, 1987), pp. 112–13.
19. 'A Time to Heal' (London, Church House Publishing, 2000), p. 1.
20. Vanessa Herrick & Ivan Mann, 1998, op. cit., pp. 36 and 40.
21. Dylan Thomas, 'Do not go gentle into that good night' in *Dylan Thomas, Collected Poems 1934–53*, ed. Walford Davies and Ralph Maud (London, Everyman, 1989), p. 148.
22. Cf. John 12.
23. Ann Lewin, 1997, op. cit., p. 4.
24. See also Morris Maddocks, *The Christian Healing Ministry* (London, SPCK, 1982), pp. 198–9.

10: THE PLACE OF ENCOUNTER: OBEDIENCE AND DISCIPLESHIP

1. 'Obedience' has, of course, long been one of the three vows usually taken by members of religious communities. Here, the emphasis is on obedience as a key to peaceful community living, rather than oppressive rule by those in religious authority. The relationship between individual conscience and the corporate will of the community, however, is often a point of tension.
2. Matt. 16:16; Mark 8:29; Luke 9:20.
3. Matt. 16:24ff; Mark 8:34ff; Luke 9:23ff.
4. Matt. 17:5; Mark 9:7; Luke 9:35.
5. Matt. 3:17; cf. Mark 1:11; Luke 3:22.
6. Cf. Ps. 2:7; Isa. 42:1.
7. John 12:28.
8. John 12:30.
9. From 'I Sing the Birth' by Ben Jonson, quoted in *A Worship Anthology*

for Advent and Christmas, ed. H. J. Richards (Bury St Edmunds, Kevin Mayhew, 1994), p. 31.

10. See Ch. 3, n 18.
11. See pp. 98ff.
12. See pp. 98ff.
13. Matt. 3:16; Mark 1:10; Luke 3:22.
14. John 1:32–4.
15. Matt. 3:11; Mark 1:8; Luke 3:16; John 1:33.
16. Ramsey, 1949, op. cit., ch. 13.
17. Cf. Exod. 34:29ff.
18. 2 Cor. 3:16–18.
19. Matt. 4:1; Mark 1:12; Luke 4:1.
20. See Rowan Williams' essay in *Sounding the Depths: Theology Through the Arts* (London: SCM, 2002).
21. Eph. 1:4.
22. Phil. 2:5–11.
23. Matt. 17:1; Mark 9:2; Luke 9:28.
24. Matt. 4:18–22; Mark 1:16–20; Luke 5:1–11.
25. Luke 9:32.
26. Luke 9:32.
27. Matt. 17:4; Mark 9:5; Luke 9:33.
28. It is worth pointing out here the etymological association between the word 'obedience' and the verb 'to listen'. Both find their roots in the Latin verb *audire*, 'to hear'. Thus there is a close relation between the two, demonstrated in Scripture in such passages as Matt. 28:16–20 (the commissioning of the disciples) and Deut. 5:1–5 (Moses' declaration to the people of Israel concerning the commandments of God: 'Hear, O Israel . . . ').
29. John 1:14.
30. 1 John 1:1.
31. Rev. 1:13, 16; cf. Dan. 7:9–14.
32. Rev. 1:17; cf. Matt. 17:7: 'But Jesus came and touched them saying, "Get up and do not be afraid." '
33. Acts 4:20.
34. 2 Pet. 1:16–19.
35. Matt. 28:16.
36. Acts 1:9.
37. Matt. 28:17; Luke 24:52.
38. Matt. 28:19–20; Mark 16:15–18; Luke 24:44ff; John 20:21ff; Acts 1:8ff.
39. Acts 1:10–11.
40. Luke 7:22.
41. See p. 14, cf. p. 120.
42. Elias Chacour with Mary E. Jensen, *We Belong to the Land: The story of a Palestinian Israeli who works for Peace and Reconciliation*, 2nd edn (Indiana, University of Notre Dame Press, 2001), pp. 46–7.

11: BEYOND FACE VALUE

1. Stuart Hall, in his article 'Synoptic Transfigurations: Mark 9:2–10 and Partners' in *King's Theological Review 10.2 (1987)*, is scathing about such preaching, referring to 'that banal nonsense . . . to the effect that the coming down to the plain below is more important than what happened on the mountain; a doctrine which says more about the practical atheism of modern British religion than about the Gospel of Christ or the texts of the New Testament' (p. 41).
2. Matt. 17:2.
3. Luke 9:29.
4. See Exod. 20:4. More often, references to God's face tend to emphasise his 'presence' – as in the 'bread of the presence' or 'showbread' (KJV) kept in the holy place, the same word *panim* being used to mean both.
5. Gen. 32:30.
6. Exod. 33:20.
7. 1 Kings 19:13.
8. Gen. 33:10.
9. Exod. 34:29ff.
10. St Bonaventure's *Life of St Francis* in *The Little Flowers of St Francis, The Mirror of Perfection, St Bonaventure's Life of St Francis* (London, J. M. Dent & Sons, 1976), p. 396.
11. Acts 6:5.
12. Acts 6:8.
13. Acts 6:15.
14. Acts 8:55–6.
15. Acts 9:1–18.
16. Or Tabor.
17. Ramsey, 1949, op. cit., pp. 127, 146.
18. See p. 149.

INDEX